This book is the property of:

. . . .

College/School . . . .

Technology of Skilled Processes

Basic Engineering Competences

Soft Soldering, Hard Soldering and Brazing

Editorial Panel

J Braddock, CEng, MWeldl, MISME, Cert Ed
Head of Fabrication and Welding Studies
W R Tuson College, Preston

K Walker, TEng(CEI), MISME, AWeldl, Cert Ed
Lecturer in Fabrication and Welding Studies
W R Tuson College, Preston

V Green, TEng(CEI), MBIM
Head of Department of Engineering Crafts
Huddersfield Technical College

C Sutcliffe, OBE, MSc, CEng, MIMechE
Vocational Curriculum Services
City and Guilds of London Institute

Published as a
co-operative venture
between
Stam Press Ltd

 and

City and Guilds

Syllabus

Technology of Skilled Processes 367-1

Section	Process	Section	Process
1	Observing Safe Practices	8	Joining
2	Moving Loads	9	Fabrication
3	Measurement and Dimensional Control (1)	10	Soft Soldering, Hard Soldering and Brazing
4	Marking Out	11	Fusion Welding
5	Work and Toolholding	12	Power Transmission
6	Removing Material	13	Assembly and Dismantling (1)
7	Forming	14	Interpreting Drawings, Specifications and Da

Syllabus

Basic Engineering Competences 201

Basic Engineering Technology
201-1-01
01 Industrial Studies
02 Observing Safe Practices
03 Moving Loads
04 Measurement and Dimensional Control (1)
05 Marking Out
06 Work and Toolholding
07 Removing Material
08 Joining
09 Interpreting Drawings. Specifications and Data
010 Assembly and Dismantling (1)

Basic Fabrication and Welding Technology
201-1-07
01 Forming
02 Fabrication
03 Soft Soldering, Hard Soldering and Brazing
04 Fusion Welding

Basic Maintenance Technology
201-1-09
01 Forming
02 Soft Soldering, Hard Soldering and Brazing
03 Power Transmission
04 Measurement and Testing of Electro-Mechanical Systems (1)

Science Background to Technology
201-1-04
01 Basic Physical Quantities, Electricity and Magneti
02 Forces
03 Pressure
04 The Principles of Tool Construction; Materials Technology

SUPPORTING BOOKS

Book titles	Covering	Coverin
Basic Engineering	**Syllabus** 367-1	Syllabus 201-1-0
Observing Safe Practices and Moving Loads	Sections 1 and 2	02-03
Measuring and Marking Out	Sections 3 and 4	04-05
Workholding and Toolholding, Removing Material	Sections 5 and 6	06-07
Joining	Section 8	08
Interpreting Drawings, Specifications and Data	Section 14	09
Assembling and Dismantling	Section 13	10
Fabrication and Welding		Syllabus 201-1-07
Forming	Section 7	01
Fabrication	Section 9	02
Soft Soldering, Hard Soldering and Brazing	Section 10	03
Fusion Welding	Section 11	04
Maintenance		Syllabus 201-1-09
Forming	Section 7	01
Soft Soldering, Hard Soldering and Brazing	Section 10	02
Power Transmission	Section 12	03
Science		Syllabus 201-1-04
Basic Physical Quantities, Electricity and Magnetism		01
Forces		02
Pressure		03
Principles of Tool Construction; Material Technology		04

201 – Basic Engineering Competences
201-1-07 Basic Fabrication and Welding Technology

03 Basic competence in Soft Soldering, Hard Soldering and Brazing

The contents of this book have been designed to cover the requirements of the City and Guilds Basic Process Competence Syllabus (367-1), section 10. The contents of component 03 of the City and Guilds Basic Engineering Technology Syllabus 201-1-07 are identical and thus equally covered by this book.

As listed, the heading references in this book conform with those in the syllabus section 10 of scheme 367-1. In the 201 scheme syllabus items are numbered consecutively and prefixed with the component number, e.g. item 1 in syllabus 03 is 3.1.

Below, in brackets following the page numbers, we give the 201 syllabus sequence numbers.

Contents Soft Soldering, Hard Soldering and Brazing

Acknowledgements

The publishers gladly record their thanks to the following contributors who have kindly supplied material for inclusion in this book:

Longman Group Ltd, who allowed the use of material from *Fabrication and Welding*, by W Kenyon; J and W Hall Ltd; Johnson Matthey and Company; The Copper Development Association; Sifbronze Ltd; Waltons of Ratcliffe; T M T Design Ltd; Huntingdon Fusion Techniques Ltd; The British Oxygen Company Ltd; The British Standards Institution; The Engineering Industry Training Board.

This book is intended for those who are, or will be, doing a practical job in industry.

It is specially written for those who need their technology as a background to their work and as a means of adapting to changes in working practices caused by technological advance. Where words such as 'he' or 'craftsman' appear in this series, they are to be interpreted as 'he/she', 'craftsman/craftswoman'.

This new series of textbooks presents the technology in terms of competence rather than working from a conventional theoretical base, i.e. the material will help readers understand:
- the use of
- the change to
- the development of
- other uses of

industrial process technology and skills.

This book has been compiled after a survey of the industrial skilled processes which form the nucleus of occupational schemes and pre-vocational courses of the City and Guilds of London Institute and a comparison with provisions elsewhere in Europe.

Three basic facts emerged:
- the technology is common to many different schemes though the contexts of applications are very different;
- the technology is being taught in a variety of workshops in a variety of exercises related to the immediate needs of students and their industries; these industrially-related exercises formed excellent learning tasks and provided clear motivation for students because of their immediate relevance;
- the technology is so well integrated with the 'first-task need' that students did not recognise its relevance to many other tasks they would be called upon to perform.

This book seeks to build on the learning tasks and to provide a means of learning and generalising the technology, so that the immediate job is better understood and better done, new tasks using the same process technology are more quickly mastered and updating or retraining is easier and more effective.

The editors are grateful to those organisations mentioned in the Acknowledgements who provided help and encouragement in the production of this book. They would also welcome further constructive suggestions, which should be addressed to:

Stam Press Ltd
Old Station Drive
Leckhampton
Cheltenham
GL53 0DN

First published in Great Britain 1987
as a co-operative venture between Stam Press Ltd and the City and Guilds of London Institute

Reprinted 1989

© Stam Press Ltd, Cheltenham, 1987

ISBN 085973 029 8

Printed and bound in Great Britain by Martin's of Berwick

1 Soldering and brazing

Introduction

A method of joining two metals together by raising their temperature has been known since ancient times. In Egypt around the year 1500 BC a brazing process was used in the manufacture of jewellery.

1.a Purpose

The purpose of making a joint by either soldering or brazing is to create a permanent non-fusion joint between two or more metal components using a metallic agent.

The term 'soldering' describes the hot joining of metals by adhesion using, as a thin film between the parts to be joined, a metallic bonding alloy having a relatively low melting point.

The term 'brazing' is a general term, which by tradition has been used to cover the wide range of joining processes where the parent metal is not deliberately melted and where the temperatures involved are too high for the term 'soldering' to be used.

BS 499:1983 defines brazing as:

'A process of joining generally applied to metals in which during or after heating, molten filler metal is drawn into or retained in the space between closely adjacent surfaces of the parts to be joined by capillary attraction. In general the melting point of the filler metal is above 500°C, but always below the melting temperature of the parent metal.'

Both soldering and brazing use heat to raise the temperature of the metals in order that a non-ferrous alloy having a lower melting point may be used as a filler metal.

'Hard soldering' is a term to describe what is essentially a brazing process in which the filler metal will not melt below red heat. The filler metal sometimes contains a high percentage of silver and is then termed 'silver solder'.

It must be appreciated that the mechanical strength of this type of joint is low when compared with a fusion welded joint, as full fusion does not take place.

Note: Brazing must not be confused with braze welding. Braze welding is defined by BS 499:1983 as: 'The joining of metals using a technique similar to fusion welding and a filler metal, but neither using capillary action as brazing nor intentionally melting the parent metal.'

'Bronze welding' is a term which has been used for many years, but is now outdated and misleading, as the filler alloys used are not bronze but brass. Braze welding is, therefore, the correct term to describe this type of joining.

Because the requirements of a brazed joint are different from those of a soldered joint the filler metal used has a different composition. As a result of this difference, the filler metal and subsequent joint have different characteristics and properties. For example, the tensile strength of a brazed joint is higher than that of a soldered joint, and the melting point of the filler metal for a brazed joint is higher than the melting point of the filler used when making a soldered joint.

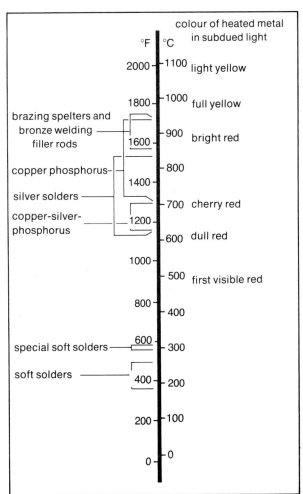

Fig. **1.1** Melting ranges of jointing materials with colour indications

Consequently more heat is required for brazing than is required for soldering (Fig. **1.**1). Although it is not always the case, as a general rule the method used to supply the heat for a brazed joint differs from that used for a soldered joint.

1.b Requirements

The requirements of the respective joints will vary according to the purpose of the joint. The following list sets out the criteria that particular joints must meet.

1.b.i–vi Criteria

- A joint container which is to hold fluids must be fluidthight.
- The joint must be strong enough to withstand any stress likely to be applied during normal usage.
- Whatever the purpose of the joint, it must be neat in appearance.
- For certain applications the joint may have to withstand the effects of heat.
- If the joint is likely to be subjected to chemical contamination it must be corrosion-resistant.
- When the joint is used in electrical work, it must have good electrical conductivity.

2 Methods used

Since the soldering and brazing processes require different temperatures in order to complete the joint it follows that the method of applying the heat will differ.

Soldering

The lower temperature requirement of the soft soldering process allows the use of indirect heat, e.g. a soldering iron (Fig. **2.**1). The copper bit is heated in a flame, or – as in the case of an electric soldering iron – by an internally housed heating element, and is then applied to the joint area, where heat transfer takes place.

The method described above is the most commonly used in small workshops or DIY applications. However, three further methods are used in industrial applications:

- applying the naked flame to the joint
- dip soldering
- heating by non-contact techniques.

The hard soldering process requires a higher temperature; this is commonly achieved by the use of a blowpipe – gas and air – or a carbon arc where an electric current, in the form of arc between a carbon rod electrode and the workpiece, provides the heat needed to complete the process.

Brazing

The brazing process requires a higher temperature than that used for soldering (Fig. **2.**2).

In general applications, small workshops and DIY, a flame directed on to the joint area is the source of heat. However, in the more sophisticated applications used in industry, heating for the brazing process may be provided by:

- a high frequency (HF) induction coil
- a gas, oil or electrically-heated closed furnace.

When the induction coil or closed furnace is used the joint surfaces are pre-treated with flux.

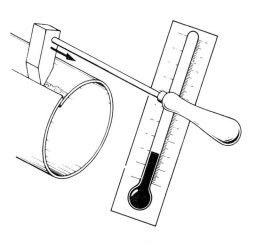

Fig. **2.**1   Soldering and relative temperature

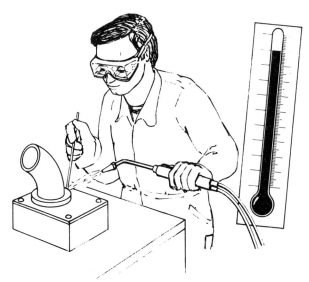

Fig. **2.**2   Brazing and relative temperature

3 Forms of heating and heating equipment used

This section explains the methods of obtaining the necessary temperature and outlines the equipment used to provide the heating in the soldering and brazing processes.

3.a Directly and indirectly heated soldering irons

The soldering iron is used for the manual soldering of joints in sheet metal and for connections in electrical wiring. The copper bit of the soldering iron, because of the nature of copper, has a high thermal conductivity and has good 'wetting' properties (i.e. 'tins' without difficulty: 'wetting' is fully explained in Section 8.c).

3.a.i Directly heated soldering irons

The directly heated iron (Fig. **3.**1) must be held in a flame until the copper bit is hot enough to ensure that when the iron is removed from the flame and applied to the joint area a soldered joint can be completed. The soldering iron quickly releases its heat and cools, making re-heating necessary. During the iron re-heat time, the joint cools and when a large joint is being made, this repeated heating, cooling and re-heating of the joint can result in imperfections. To overcome this, a gas-heated soldering stove (Fig. **3.**2) in which two irons are heated is sometimes used.

3.a.ii Indirectly heated (electric) soldering irons

The electric soldering iron (Figs. **3.**3 and **3.**4) is widely used for making joints in electric circuitry. The heating element contained in the barrel of the iron is supplied directly from the mains electrical supply, or, for small low-power irons, a lower voltage from a mains transformer.

3.b Flame heating

The oxy-fuel gas flame is .widely used when torch brazing, but for the relatively low temperature needed when brazing it is often more economical to use a gas torch, where the acetylene is replaced with natural gas and the oxygen with air.

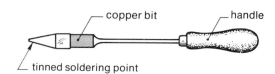

Fig. **3.**1   Soldering iron — requiring external heating

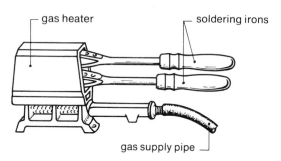

Fig. **3.**2   Soldering irons and gas heater

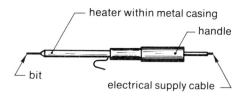

Fig. **3.**3   Electric soldering iron (lightweight) 25 watt

Fig. 3.4   Electric soldering iron — oval tapered bit 125 wa

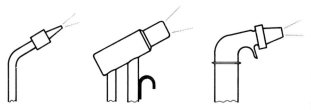

Fig. 3.5   Nozzle profiles

Fig. **3.**6 A multi-station fixed torch rotary brazing table

Fig. **3.**7 Induction brazing equipment

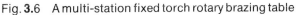

The torch must be designed to suit the gases used as it is important to obtain the correct gas mixtures for full combustion (Fig. **3.**5). Flame brazing is one of the most commonly used methods of brazing.

There is a wide range of equipment available, from the simple gas torch operated manually to fully automated gas torch assemblies. These often include special jigs for pre-loading the joints to be brazed, timing devices to prevent overheating of the components and other items of equipment to assist in quality control.

To conserve heat when brazing small components, firebricks can be arranged to form a screen and to provide a platform on which the component can be placed.

A modification of manual torch brazing is fixed torch brazing. With this method one or more torches are fixed into position and the workpiece is moved past the torch flame. The workpiece could be moved mechanically by means of a conveyor belt or by being placed on a turntable (Fig. **3.**6). This method of heating is suitable for batch production for batches of fifty to one hundred. Where mass production is required for larger quantities, sophisticated industrial techniques have been developed.

3.c High frequency (HF) induction heating

In this method of heating a water-cooled coil, supplied with a high frequency alternating current, provides the energy to generate heat in the components to be brazed. The component is placed within the confines of the coil, but not in contact with it (Fig. **3.**7). The high-frequency current passing through the coil generates eddy currents, which are manifested as heat, on the surface of the component. The components must be pre-fluxed and assembled with a filler alloy insert in the joint, before being placed in the coil.

3.d Furnace heating

In this method the components are also pre-fluxed and assembled, with a filler alloy insert fitted to the joint area, and then inserted into a gas, oil or electrically-heated furnace. To prevent oxidation of the component there is usually a reducing atmosphere within the furnace.

Note: A reducing atmosphere is one in which there is a deficiency of free oxygen. A reactive gas, e.g. hydrogen or carbon monoxide, is introduced into the furnace to lower the oxygen content and to prevent the entry of oxygen from the outside atmosphere.

4.a Soft soldering

There are many applications of soft soldering to be seen today. Some are given below:

4.a.i Light fabricated components

- Copper and brass fabrications for prototype and ornamental work
- Tin-plate oil can (Fig. **4**.1)
- Tin-plate cans for preserving food.

4.a.ii Pipe joints

- Joints in the copper pipes through which natural gas is piped in the home
- Joints in the copper water distribution pipes in the home (Fig. **4**.2).

4.a.iii Electrical connections

- Cable connections used in electrical engineering, telephones, radio and television equipment
- Soldered connections in mini-computers.

4.b Hard soldering and brazing

Hard soldering or brazing is used for any joint where soft soldering is not strong enough, or where the temperature around the completed joint is likely to rise to the melting point of the solder.

There are many applications of brazing:

4.b.i Fabricated components

- In fabrications where, if fusion welding were used, there would be problems with distortion

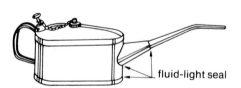

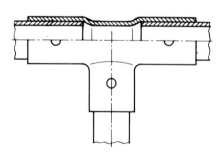

Fig. **4**.1   Oil can, an example of tin-plate fabrication

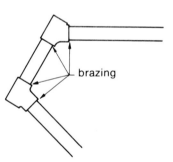

Fig. **4**.3   Joining dissimilar metals by brazing

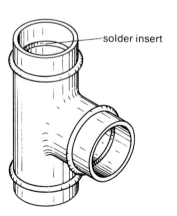

a Joint in copper water distribution

b Capillary fitting Tee connection

Fig. **4**.2   Tee connections in piping

- When joining dissimilar metals, such as brass fittings to a copper tank.

4.b.ii Pipe joints

- Joints between steel pipes and malleable cast iron fittings
- Joints in the frame of a bycicle and other tubular structures (Fig. **4.**3).

4.b.iii Cutting tools

- To secure the carbide tip to the body of a cutting tool (Fig. **4.**4).

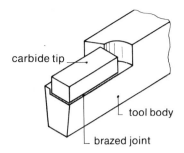

carbide tip

tool body

brazed joint

Fig. **4.**4 A carbide tip brazed on a cutting tool

5 Description of equipment, principles of operation and making a joint

5.a Soldering irons

- **Description and operation:** The soldering iron conveys heat to the joint, melts the solder and transfers it to the joint. To carry out this function efficiently the soldering iron must be capable of storing heat and, when placed in contact with the joint, of transferring the heat quickly.

  Copper, which has a good thermal conductivity, is used as the soldering bit.

  Soldering irons are available in a variety of sizes and weights with bits shaped to suit the particular application.

- **Making a solder joint using a soldering iron:** Before any soldering operation is attempted the soldering iron and the joint surfaces must be prepared (refer to Section 6.b).

  The bit of the soldering iron must be tinned, i.e. must have a film of solder covering the soldering bit.

Tinning the bit

- Heat the iron to the correct temperature (about 50°C above the melting point of the solder). A rule of thumb test for temperature is to hold the heated soldering iron approximately 10 cm away from your cheek. The heat from a correctly heated iron should be just detectable at this distance. Great care must be taken not to bring the iron into contact with your face during this test.
- Clean the bit with a file or steel wool.
- Dip the bit in a flux (refer to Section 8).
- Apply a small amount of solder to the bit and allow it to spread over and cover the tip.
- The soldering iron bit is now tinned.

After the joint surfaces have been prepared (refer to Section 6.b) apply the heated iron to the joint. Allow a little time for the transfer of heat from the iron to the joint to cause the wetted surfaces of the joint to become fluid. Add solder to the soldering iron bit. The solder will melt and flow from the iron into the joint (Fig. **5.**1). Move the iron over the area of the joint (Fig. **5.**2) adding solder as necessary.

Note: Too much solder will lead to a lumpy, weak joint. Remove the soldering iron and allow the joint to cool. Clean any flux residue from the joint area. Provided the joint has been assembled with a very

small gap, capillary action will cause the solder to penetrate the full width of the joint (this action is fully explained in Section 6.c). The layer of solder will react with the parent metal and form an intermetallic compound between the parent metal and the layer of solder. This compound is an important factor and contributes to the strength of the joint as it is stronger than the solder itself (Fig. **5.**3). The completed joint should be cooled fairly quickly, because holding the

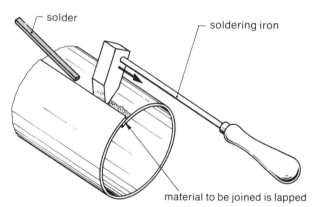

Fig. **5.**1   A soldered joint being made

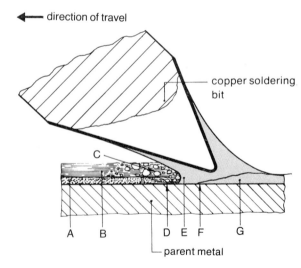

A oxide film on parent metal
B flux solution above oxidised metal surface
C boiling flux solution removing oxide film
D bare metal in contact with fused flux
E liquid solder
F tin reacting with base metal to form intermetallic compound
G solidifying solder

Fig. **5.**2   A soft soldered joint being made

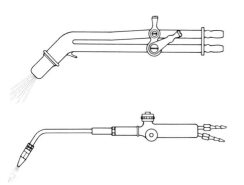

Fig. **5.3** Section through a soft-soldered lap joint

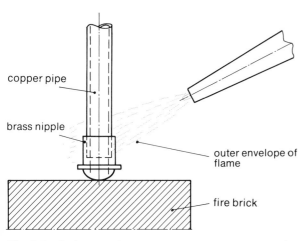

Fig. **5.4** Gas torches for soft soldering and brazing

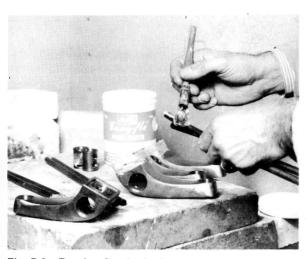

copper pipe

brass nipple

outer envelope of flame

fire brick

Fig. **5.5** Soft soldering a brass nipple to a copper pipe

Fig. **5.6** Brazing flux in the form of a paste

joint at a high temperature for a long period will cause the formation of a thick layer of compound which will reduce the strength of the joint.

After the joint has been completed and cooled the flux residue must be removed or corrosion will result. This may be done by washing the joint in hot water which contains a few drops per litre of hydrochloric acid. This acid solution must then be neutralised by rinsing in a alkaline solution of hot water and soda crystals.

5.b Gas torches

- **Description and operation:** Gas torches (Fig. **5.**4) are used to apply heat to the joint area and are designed to be used with specific gas mixtures such as *natural gas and air* or *oxygen and propane*, etc. The gases are supplied via hoses to the torch, the flow rates being adjustable by the two mixer controls on the torch body. The resultant flammable mix of gas is burnt at the torch nozzle.

  Note: It is dangerous to use gas torch with gases other than those for which it was designed.

- **Making a joint using a torch:** The procedure used when making various joints using a gas torch is as follows:

- A *soft soldered joint:* Making a soft soldered joint using a gas torch can be better explained if we look at the specific example of joining a brass nipple to a copper pipe. As with soldering using a soldering iron, the joint surfaces must be prepared before any attempts to join the parts. We then proceed as follows:

  (a) Assemble the two components in the vertical position (Fig. **5.**5). Heat loss can be avoided if the work is placed on a firebrick.

  (b) Direct the outer envelope of the flame on to the joint area, heating the full length of the brass nipple.

  (c) When the temperature of the workpiece is correct, just above the melting point of the solder, remove the flame and apply the tin-lead solder carefully to the joint edge between the nipple and the pipe. Capillary action will ensure that the solder will flow through the joint.

  (d) After the joint has cooled clean it by washing, as described in Section 5.a.

- A *brazed joint:* When a brazed joint is made, the parts to be joined must first be cleaned and fluxed (refer to Section 6.b). A paste flux (Fig. **5.**6) is applied, after which the parts are assembled, the lap joint having a small gap. This small gap is essential for capillary action to take place.

To avoid heat loss the workpiece may be placed on a firebrick (Fig. **5.**7).

An oxidising flame – refer to the series book *Fusion Welding* – should be used to heat the workpiece. The flame should be larger than that used for fusion welding, but only the outer envelope of the flame should be brought into contact with the joint area. An oxidising flame is used to counteract the tendency of the zinc content of the filler metal to vaporise and so cause porosity in the joint.

When the joint is at the correct temperature, i.e. just above the melting point of the brazing filler alloy, the flux will begin to melt into a thin liquid. The flame should be moved along the joint while the filler rod, unless flux coated, is heated and dipped into a powdered flux. The filler rod should then be applied to the hot metal of the joint area, taking care to ensure that it *does not enter the flame*.

Filler metal, melted by the temperature of the joint area, will flow into, and fill the gap and run slightly ahead. This procedure is repeated until the joint is completed.

When the completed joint has cooled to room temperature, the flux residue must be removed. As most fluxes are soluble in water, this residue may be removed by using a wire brush and hot water. Other methods are: filing, grinding, sand or shot-blasting.

It takes considerable practice to acquire the skill needed to make a sound brazed joint.

- *Braze welded joints:* To braze weld a joint a different method is employed from that used when making a brazed joint. The joint should first be prepared so that a fillet of deposited filler metal can be made along the joint. Then work in the following stages:
  - (a) Adjust the torch flame for a slightly oxidising flame (Fig. **5.**8).
  - (b) Heat the filler rod and dip it into the borax-based flux. This operation will need to be repeated several times.
  - (c) Apply the flame so that the tip of the inner blue cone is almost in contact with the joint area.
  - (d) When it is judged that the correct temperature has been reached, apply the filler rod to the joint and ensure that a globule of molten filler metal is deposited.
  - (e) Repeat the procedure as the weld progresses towards the left (assuming a leftward technique). If a circular motion of the torch flame is used and careful control of the filler globules maintained, a neat fillet of the filler metal will be deposited along the joint.

5.c High frequency induction heating

In induction brazing, the method of supplying the heat to the workpiece is different from that previously described.

When the joint is heated with a brazing torch, a welding torch or by a gas-heated furnace, the heat is always applied to the joint from the outside. With induction heating the heat is generated in the workpiece itself. The principle of induction brazing is as follows:

If a coil carrying a high-frequency alternating current is placed around or within a component (Figs. **5.**9 and **5.**10) eddy currents will be set up in the surface of the component. These eddy currents create the heat energy required to complete the brazing process (Fig. **5.**11). The frequency of the currents used may be vary between 1 kHz and 1 MHz.

The application of a very high frequency current for a very short time confines the heating effect to a thin layer on the surface of the workpiece. However, when lower frequencies are used for longer periods of time, the heat will penetrate deeper into the material. Because brazing requires considerable heat penetration, the frequency used is in the order of 5 kHz. When this method of brazing is used the joint is assembled with a pre-placed insert of filler alloy (Fig. **5.**12); these inserts are available in a variety of shapes and sizes (Fig. **5.**13).

During high frequency brazing the heating cycle – temperature and time – is fully controlled. The process may be carried out in a reducing atmosphere, where the formation of oxide is prevented and it is not necessary to use a flux.

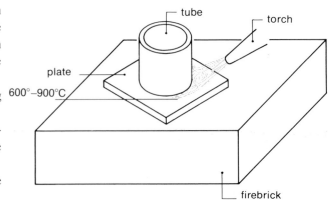

Fig. **5.**7   Brazing a brass tube to a brass plate

note: very short pointed cone

Fig. **5.**8   Oxidising flame

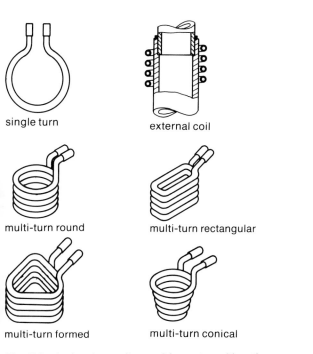

single turn

external coil

multi-turn round

multi-turn rectangular

multi-turn formed

multi-turn conical

Fig. **5**.9   Induction coils used for external heating

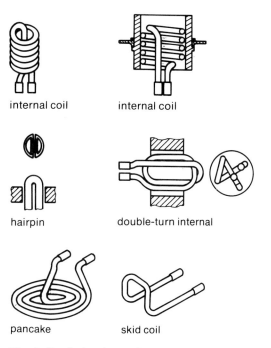

internal coil

internal coil

hairpin

double-turn internal

pancake

skid coil

Fig. **5**.10   Induction coils used for internal heating and flat surfaces

Fig. **5**.11   Tungsten carbide tips for induction brazing tips on to rotary drilling bits

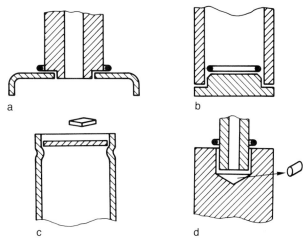

a

b

c

d

a Wire ring sited for HF induction heating
b Wire ring sited for torch, induction or furnace heating
c A case where a ring should be used for a large diameter or a slug for up to about 8 mm diameter
d A case for either ring or slug. If a slug is used the rod must fall freely into the hole. It should have a groove or flat for venting.

Fig. **5**.12   Methods of pre-placing alloy

The components to be brazed are first cleaned, fluxed if required and assembled with an insert of filler alloy before being placed in the induction coil.

This process is essentially one which would be used on fairly long production runs. The handling costs may be reduced by using a device which will automatically position the assembled components inside the induction coil. The removal or ejection of the brazed component should also be an automatic operation.

The main disadvantage of this method is the rather expensive electrical equipment which is needed.

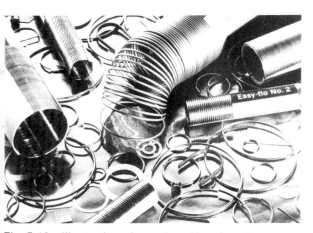

Fig. **5**.13   Illustration of pre-placed brazing alloys

5.d Furnace brazing

Furnace brazing is particularly economical when large numbers of components are to be brazed and is suitable for the fabrication of small to medium-sized components (Fig. **5.**14). This process is also ideal for brazing parts which are likely to distort through localised heating, as in torch brazing. Very high rates of output and uniformly good results can be achieved with relatively unskilled operators.

Two main types of furnace are discussed.

Dry furnaces

These may be heated by gas or electricity; the components to be brazed are placed on racks in the furnace. An inert gas or a reducing atmosphere may be introduced into the furnace to protect the parts from oxidation (Fig. **5.**14b), in which case there will be no need to pickle after brazing.

Note: Pickling is the process during which any scale is removed from the surface of the brazed joint by the application of a dilute solution of sulphuric acid.

Where a flux is necessary when brazing in the controlled atmosphere of a furnace, less needs to be used than if the brazing were to be carried out in air. As with induction brazing, the filler alloy must be pre-placed in the joint. Control of the temperature in the furnace is essential.

It is possible to use what is known as a *continuous furnace*. Here the components are fed through the temperature-controlled furnace at a pre-determined rate and quickly reach the temperature required to ensure that the filler alloy flows through the joints. This method avoids over-heating. Conveyor belt furnaces are preferred for brazing small to medium-sized parts, especially when large production runs are required. The advantage of these furnaces is that they can be made part of the production line.

The prepared components, assembled with filler alloy inserts, are placed on a heat-resistant conveyor belt which passes through the furnace. Lightweight parts to be brazed, e.g. electric contacts and products of the jewellery industry, are placed on smooth belts made of high-alloy heat-resisting strip steel. The speed of the belt should be such that the components are held for only two to three minutes at brazing temperature. This is quite enough for the filler alloy to fill the entire joint gap.

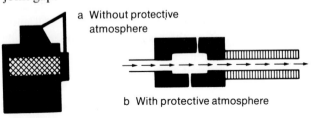

a Without protective atmosphere

b With protective atmosphere

Fig. **5.**14 Furnace for brazing – muffle furnace

Salt bath furnaces

These furnaces, which may be heated by gas or electricity, consist of a suitably shaped vessel containing molten salt in which the components to be joined are immersed.

Advantages: the components are heated quickly and evenly because they are immersed in the liquid salt. No oxidation will occur, because air is excluded, and very accurate temperature control is possible.

Disadvantages: the furnaces are expensive, the components cannot be viewed during the process and some of the salt will adhere to the component and drip off during subsequent handling.

In this process the component parts must be assembled complete with the filler alloy insert before being placed in the salt bath.

5.e Resistance brazing

In this method of brazing a high current at low voltage is passed through the parts to be joined or via electrodes clamped to the component parts (Fig. **5.**15).

Any resistance to the passage of an electric current gives rise to power loss, manifested as heat, i.e. the areas of high resistance will be heated.

The highest resistance to the passage of the electric

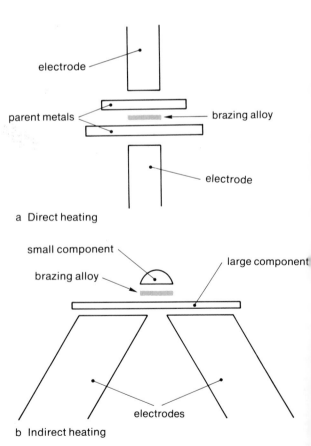

electrode

parent metals

brazing alloy

electrode

a Direct heating

small component

large component

brazing alloy

electrodes

b Indirect heating

Fig. **5.**15 Assembly of components for resistance brazing

current through the components to be joined will be at the joint interface and, therefore, as the current flows through the joint the temperature will rise. By control of the current flow, the temperature of the joint can be controlled to bring it to the brazing temperature and maintain it there. Normally a flux is needed with this method of brazing; the filler alloy is either hand-fed or pre-placed in the joint.

This process is only suitable for relatively small joint areas since it is difficult to achieve a uniform current distribution across the joint. The application of resistance brazing techniques to the production of assemblies can often result in very high rates of output.

5.f Dip brazing

In this method of brazing either the whole assembly or the joint area of the components to be joined is immersed in a bath of molten brazing alloy in order to bring the joint area to the brazing temperature and to complete the process. The brazing alloy is drawn into the joint gap by capillary attraction, the flow being assisted if the workpiece is repeatedly raised and lowered. The molten brazing alloy is protected from oxidation by a layer of flux which floats on the surface.

When the assembly is removed from the molten alloy bath, all but a very thin layer of alloy will drip from the surface. This thin layer may be removed by mechanical means or electrolytically.

As with all brazed joints, the surface must be cleaned before assembly. Since the process relies upon capillary attraction to make a sound joint, great care must be used when assembling the joint to ensure that the joint gap is correct.

The process is usually limited to small components and requires considerable operator skill, since manual operation is fairly difficult to control.

6 Working principles of soft solders and filler alloys

6.a Melting points of elements and alloys

Soft solders

There are many different types of solder, each formulated for use in a particular type of application. Table **6.**1 lists and comments on thirteen different types of solder.

All soft solders are based on an alloy of tin and lead; other elements, such as antimony and silver, are sometimes included to give additional characteristics, as explained later.

The melting point of a solder is of prime importance. Tin has a melting point of 232°C and lead has a melting point of 327°C. When the two metals are alloyed as a solder the melting point of the resulting substance is lower than that of either tin or lead. The ratio of tin to lead in the alloy determines the melting point. For instance, when a molten alloy containing 90 per cent tin and 10 per cent lead is cooled, the alloy reaches a temperature of 216°C before it begins to solidify. As the alloy cools further it slowly changes from a fluid state to a plastic state before it completely solidifies at a temperature of 183°C. At the other end of the order an alloy containing 20 per cent tin and 80 per cent lead will start to freeze at a temperature of 280°C and completely solidify at 183°C, indicating a temperature range between melting point and freezing point. By consulting Fig. **6.**1 it can be seen that tin–lead alloys containing between 19.5 and 97.5 per cent tin reach full solidification at a temperature of 183°C.

It is fortunate that this phenomenon makes it possible to produce on the one hand a soft solder which will solidify quickly, and on the other hand one which will solidify slowly. In the first group, one particular alloy containing 62 per cent tin and 38 per cent lead melts and solidifies entirely at 183°C. This alloy is known as the 'eutectic' alloy and its 'eutectic temperature' is

Table 6.1 List of selected soft solders — ecxtracted from BS 219: 1977

Description	Average composition			Approx. melting range	Remarks
	Tin	Antimony	Lead		
	max %	max %	%	°C	
A	64·0	0·6	35·4	183-185	Lowest melting range. Solder suitable for electrical, radio and instrument assemblies
K	60·0	0·5	39·5	183-188	
B	50·0	3·0	47·0	185-204	Coppersmith's bit soldering.
F	50·0	0·5	49·5	183-212	
M	45·0	2·7	52·3	185-215	
C	40·0	2·4	57·6	185-227	Blowpipe soldering.
G	40·0	0·4	59·6	183-234	
L	32·0	1·9	66·1	185-243	Long melting range.
D	32·0	1·8	68·2	185-248	
J	30·0	0·3	69·7	185-255	
Higher temperature solder	95·0	5·0	—	236-243	More difficult to use than normal solders.
		Silver %			Covered by British Patent Specifications.
	5·0	1·5	93·5	296-301	More difficult to use than normal solder.
	1·0	1·5	97·5	309-310	

183°C. At the other end of the alloy range, a solder containing 34 per cent tin and 66 per cent lead will melt at a temperature of 243°C and solidify at a temperature of 183°C. This solder is used by plumbers to make a wiped joint in lead pipe; it allows the plumber time to form the joint while the solder is in a plastic form.

Use of Table 6.1: The addition of antimony to a solder has the effect of adding strength to the joint, but it also raises the melting point. As can be seen, most soft solders contain antimony. It follows then that if a melting point of 183°C – 188°C is required a solder with a very low antimony content must be used.

Five solders of this type are listed in the table but only types A and K, because of the ratio of tin to lead, have a low melting point.

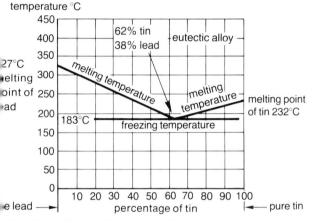

Fig. **6**.1   The melting point of tin–lead alloys

Filler alloys

The filler alloys used in the brazing, braze welding and silver soldering processes have a higher melting range than any of the soft solders previously mentioned. While the highest melting point encountered with a soft solder is around 300°C, the lowest melting point of brazing alloy is around 550°C. British Standards state that brazing is a process in which molten filler metal is drawn by capillary attraction into the space between the joint faces of the parts to be joined and that the melting point of the filler metal is always below that of the parent metal.

Modern brazing technology is based on this principle and it must be understood that there is a big difference between capillary brazing and both fusion welding and braze welding.

One of the main differences is in the joint design. Fig. **6**.2 shows how components are arranged for braze welding while Fig. **6**.3 shows the design of joints for brazing. It will be seen that in Fig. **6**.3 a lap or joint face is provided to enable the molten filler alloy to be drawn into the joint gap by capillary attraction.

Many filler alloys have been developed for brazing to meet the following requirements:

- achieving good brazing practice
- producing good capillary attraction
- melting at the right temperature
- offering resistance to corrosion
- producing the necessary strength of joint.

When selecting a filler alloy for brazing, consideration must be given to the compatibility between the chosen filler and the parent material, otherwise a poor joint will be the result.

BS 1845: 1984 *Filler Metals for Brazing* lists the filler alloys which are available under the headings shown in Table **6**.2.

Table 6.2   Brazing alloys and melting ranges

Group	Brazing alloys	Melting range °C
Group AL	Aluminium brazing	535°– 630°
Group AG	Silver brazing	600°– 800°
Group CP	Copper–phosphorus brazing	640°– 800°
Group CU	Copper brazing	1045°–1085°
Group CZ	Brazing brasses	870°– 980°
Group NI	Nickel and cobalt brazing	875°–1150°
Group PD	Palladium-bearing brazing	805°–1235°
Group AU	Gold-bearing brazing	905°–1020°

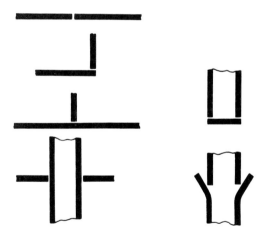

Fig. **6**.2   Joint designs for braze welding

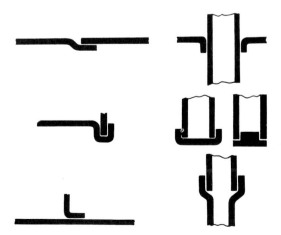

Fig. **6**.3   Joint designs for brazing

The more commonly used filler alloys are the brazing brasses and the silver brazing alloys.

It must be appreciated that neither of these can be used to join together aluminium or its alloys. In such cases the aluminium brazing alloys should be used.

Selection of a suitable brazing alloy for the particular application, from the large range available, is determined by the following requirements:

- parent metal material
- process to be used
- strength of joint required
- resistance to corrosion
- final colour of filler alloy.

Table **6**.3 lists a number of brazing brasses which are available. These are widely used when steels are brazed and, to a lesser extent, for the brazing of copper and copper alloys, the melting points of which are very nearly 1050°C.

Additives to brazing alloys

The following additives are sometimes mixed into the brazing brass:

- **silver** to improve fluidity and strength
- **silicon** to act as a deoxidant
- **nickel and manganese** to improve the strength.

When silver is an important constituent of a brazing alloy, the alloy is often called 'silver solder'. Table **6**.4 lists a range of silver solders, their components and applications.

From this table you can see that the melting point of the silver solders varies from 620°C at the lower end of the range to 855°C at the upper end.

Filler metal for braze weld joints

Silicon bronze is used as a filler alloy in this process. It is basically a copper–zinc alloy of the 60/40 class to which has been added a number of elements which act as deoxidants and toughening elements. The melting temperature is 875°C.

The inclusion of any oxide in the filler alloy is detrimental to the welding property. The use of deoxidising elements ensures that oxide is not included and that when the filler alloy melts no zinc oxide fumes, which will cause loss of zinc and porosity, are generated.

This particular filler alloy is recommended for the braze welding of brass and copper in sheet or tube form.

Other filler metals, still basically copper–zinc alloys, used in the braze welding process include manganese bronze with a melting temperature of 895°C and nickel bronze with a melting temperature of 910°C.

6.b Preparation of a surface and formation of joints

Before a soldered, brazed or braze welded joint is made, the edges of the parent material must be prepared.

Note: The depth or width of the joint should be limited to the maximum depth of penetration possible, but should not exceed 15 mm.

The joint surfaces must be free of grease and any corrosion. Vigorous rubbing with steel wool will

Table 6.3 Approximate data relating to brazing brasses

Standard specification or description	Composition			Melting range
	Copper	Zinc	Other elements	
	%	%	%	°C
BS 1845 Type 8	49–51	Remainder	Total impurities 0·85	860–870
BS 1845 Type 9	53–55	Remainder	Total impurities 0·85	870–880
BS 1845 Type 10	59–61	Remainder	Total impurities 0·90	885–890
BS 1845 Type 11	53–55	Remainder	0·8–1·2 Sn and total impurities 0·80	860–870
BS 1845 Type 12	59–61	Remainder	0·8–1·2 Sn and total impurities 0·80	880–890
Silicon brass	60–72	Remainder	Up to 0·5 Si	880–890
—	58–60	Remainder	Up to 1·0 Ag and 0·2 Si	880–890
—	57–63	Remainder	Up to 0·5 Si, 1 Fe, 1 Mn, 1·5 Sn	860–900
—	45–55	Remainder	0·5 Si, 0·5 Mn, 1 Fe, 7-16 Ni	860–950

Table 6.4 Approximate data relating to silver solders

Standard specification or description	Composition				Melting range metals	Suitable parent	Remarks
	Silver	Copper	Zinc	Cadmium			
	%	%	%	%	°C		
BS 1845 Type 3	49–51	14–16	15–17	18–20	620–640	Copper, alloy steels, nickel alloys	Low melting point
BS 1845 Type 4	60–62	27·5–29·5	9–11	—	690–735	Copper, brass, bronze, steel	High conductivity
BS 1845 Type 5	42–44	36–38	18·5–20·5	—	700–775	Copper, brass, bronze, steel, nickel	Used for general engineering purposes
—	17	50	33	—	790–830	Copper, brass, bronze, carbon steel	
—	24	43	33	—	740–780	Brass, bronze, nickel silver	Brazed joint can be cold worked
—	33·3	33·3	33·3	—	700–740	Brass, bronze, copper	Used for joining ornamental brass
ASTM B 73–29							
Grade 3	20	45	30	5	775–815	Copper, brass bronze, steel	
Grade 4	45	30	25	—	675–745		
Grade 6	65	20	15	—	695–720		High electrical conductivity
Grade 8	80	16	4	—	740–795	Copper, brass, steel	
—	10	52	37	1	840–855	Copper, brass, steel	

remove corrosion, while a cloth soaked with a proprietary solvent should be used to wipe away grease and dirt.

After cleaning, the joint is ready for assembly. When the joint is 'set up' for soldering or brazing a small gap must be left between the parts to be joined. The gap size is critical, since with no gap there will be no capillary attraction (refer to Section 6.c), while if the gap is too large there will again be no capillary attraction and the molten alloy is likely to escape from the joint.

The clearance of gap differs with different materials, For example:

ferrous materials – gap of 0.04 to 0.15 mm

copper and copper alloys – gap of 0.07 to 0.2 mm

The purpose of the increase in the set-up joint gap when joining copper and its alloy is to accommodate the additional alloying which takes place between the parent metal and the filler alloy. This would reduce penetration of the filler alloy into the joint unless the gap were increased.

Note: It may be necessary to apply flux to the joint surface before assembly, particularly if the joint is to be made in a normal atmosphere (refer to Section 8).

Pre-prepared soldered joints

When socket joints are made in domestic copper pipes capillary fittings may be used.

These fittings, elbows, tee connectors, etc. contain an insert of solder.

After the parts to be joined have been cleaned with steel wool and a flux has been applied, the two parts are assembled and a naked flame (the outer envelope of the flame being used) is applied to the joint area. The joint is completed when the solder is just visible at the edges of the socket joint.

Note: When drinking water is to be carried in the pipes a lead-free solder must be used, e.g. tin–silver solder.

Braze welded joints

The joint design for braze welding is totally different from that of a brazed joint. In braze welding, capillary action is not a factor, since the strength of the joint is based on the strength of the bond between the filler alloy and the parent metal and on the tensile strength of the filler alloy itself, which may be as high as 400 N/mm². Fig. 6.4 shows a range of joint preparations which are used for the braze welding of copper pipes.

Fig. **6.**4a shows a bell type butt joint suitable for all diameters and any thickness of pipe.

Fig. **6.**4b shows a branch T joint where a hole of diameter equal to that of the branch is cut in the main

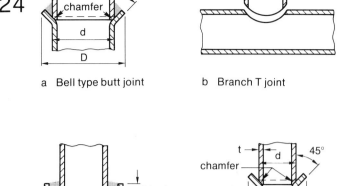

a Bell type butt joint

b Branch T joint

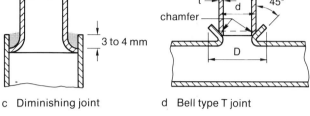

c Diminishing joint

d Bell type T joint

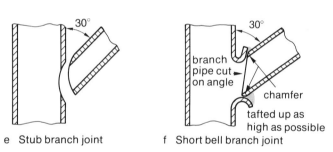

e Stub branch joint

f Short bell branch joint

Fig. **6**.4   Joint preparation for the braze welding of copper pipes

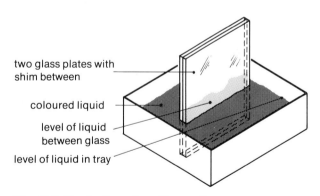

Fig. **6**.5   Illustration of capillary action

pipe and shaped to make close contact. This joint is suitable for equal and unequal branches and pipes of small diameter. It is not recommended for sanitary systems, since with a braze welded joint crevices occur, in which bacteria can collect and multiply.

Fig. **6**.4c shows a diminishing joint in which the end of the smaller pipe is 'swaged' out to fit into the larger pipe. This joint is suitable for all diameters and any thickness of pipe.

Fig. **6**.4d shows a bell-type T joint which is suitable for all diameters and any thickness of pipe.

Fig. **6**.4e shows a stub branch joint where a hole is cut in the main pipe and shaped to make close contact with the end of the branch pipe. The braze weld is completed in one operation. This joint is suitable for equal and unequal branches and for pipes of small diameter. It is not recommended for sanitary systems (see under Fig. **6**.4b).

Fig. **6**.4f shows a short bell branch joint where, after a hole has been drilled in the main pipe, the edges are 'swaged' out to form a raised cup. The branch pipe is inserted until it makes contact with the cup and the depth of insertion is at least twice the pipe thickness. This joint is suitable for all diameters and any thickness of pipe.

6.c Capillary flow

Soldering and brazing depend on capillary flow to cause the molten filler alloy to penetrate the controlled joint spaces to provide adequate jount strength.

Experiment to demonstrate capillary action

Capillary action may be observed if two pieces of clear glass (as used in electric welding shields as cover glasses) are clamped together with a shim of 0.2 mm between them to provide a gap (Fig. **6**.5). The edges of the glass plates containing the gap may now be placed in a dish containing coloured water, to a depth of 12 mm. The coloured water will be seen to rise up the gap between the glass plates to a height which is greater than 12 mm. This phenomenon is called capillary action, which will also occur in a soldered joint when the size of the gap is correct. If you repeat this experiment a number of times, using a different thickness of shim, you will see that the size of the gap between the faces of the two glass plates controls the flow of liquid between them.

Practical considerations for capillary flow

The conditions in the experiment are also true for soft soldered and brazed joints. With a gap of between 0.04 mm and 0.2 mm capillary flow will take place. However, should a wider gap of, say, 0.5 mm be used, capillary flow would be reduced and the depth of penetration of the filler alloy would be small. This would, of course, reduce the strength of the completed joint.

Causes of discontinuity in capillary flow

As has already been stated, the joint faces must be clean before the joint is made.

Although the use of a flux will help to prevent

oxidation of the joint faces, note that fluxes cannot be relied upon to remove significant amounts of contaminants; abrasive materials such as steel wool or abrasive powders should therefore be used to clean the joint faces. Degreasing should follow. This may be carried out by immersion in a solvent, either in liquid or vapour form.

Freshly cleaned metal surfaces will tarnish or oxidise very quickly in a damp or humid atmosphere. The joining process, therefore, should follow as soon as possible after the cleaning operation. If some oxide forms on the cleaned surfaces, or if some grease comes into contact with the cleaned surface before the joint is made, the result will be a lack of continuity in the capillary flow of the filler alloy. This will occur whether it is soft solder or a brazing alloy.

6.d Strength of joints

Soft solder

The tensile strength of a soft solder is determined by two factors – the composition of the solder and the temperature.

Composition: The higher the percentage tin content of the solder, the greater the tensile strength, i.e.
- A solder of 50 per cent tin, 50 per cent lead has a tensile strength of 45 N/mm² at normal temperatures.
- A solder of 60 per cent tin, 40 per cent lead has a tensile strength of 53 N/mm² at normal temperatures.

Temperature: The variation of tensile strength with temperature is best illustrated with an example:
- A solder with a composition of 60 per cent tin, 40 per cent lead will be at its highest tensile strength (130 N/mm²) at a temperature of −50°C. As the temperature increases, the tensile strength falls rapidly until at +20°C (normal temperature) the tensile strength will be 53 N/mm².

Intermetallic compound: The tensile strength of a soft soldered joint is also affected by the thickness of the solder. A chemical reaction takes place at the junction of the solder and the metal to which it adheres, which leads to the formation of an intermetallic compound. This compound has a tensile strength greater than the solder itself. Therefore a joint having a thin solder layer is likely to consist almost entirely of intermetallic compound with a higher tensile strength than a joint with a thick layer of solder where the tensile strength will be that of the solder.

Technique employed: The use of the correct soldering technique, therefore, has a direct bearing on the strength of the soldered joint. Factors that must be considered are:
- soundness of the deposited solder
- good 'wetting' of the metal
- use of the correct flux
- correct gap between joint faces
- use of sufficient heat to allow the solder to flow freely.

Brazed joints

The strength requirements for a brazed joint are similar to those for a soft soldered joint. There are, however, a number of different factors that need to be considered. These are:
- the filler alloy
- the heat required to melt the filler alloy
- the type of flux needed.

Strength of the filler metal: The tensile strength of the brass filler alloy in the 'as-cast' condition is in the order of 400 N/mm². However, by adding silver to the alloy a tensile strength of 700 N/mm² can be achieved.

Technique employed: The strength of a brazed joint depends not only on the strength of the filler metal, but on the soundness of the technique used when brazing and in the design of the joint.

The following factors must be considered:
- **Joint design**: Most brazing alloys will, under ideal conditions, penetrate a joint to a distance of 12 mm and in some cases 50 mm. However, because of costs, excessive penetration is not desirable, nor is it necessary for achieving a full-strength joint. As a general rule, a lap joint of three to four times the thickness of the thickest part of the joint is sufficient.

  To achieve optimum strength a joint must be designed to ensure an adequate area of contact between filler alloy and parent metal and to introduce shear loading as well as tension to the filler alloy (Fig. **6**.6). For example Fig. **6**.7 shows a

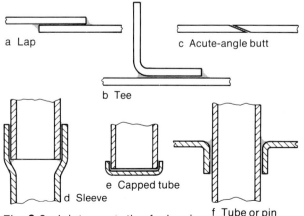

Fig. **6**.6 Joint preparation for brazing

brazed butt joint where the filler alloy is in tension only. The strength of the joint would be improved if it could be as the lap joint in Fig. **6.**6a, where the filler alloy is loaded in shear as well as tension and where full advantage is taken of the surface area of bond between brazing alloy and parent metal.

Fig. **6.**7   Filler alloy in tension (butt joint)

- **Preparation and technique**: The basic require-ments for a sound joint remain the same for a brazed joint as for a soldered joint: a clean, oxide-free joint surface, a good wetting action of the filler alloy, a controlled joint gap to assist in capillary flow and a deposit of filler alloy which is sound and free from porosity and lack of bonding.

Braze welded joints

The strength of a braze welded joint depends on:

- the filler alloy–parent metal bond
- the soundness of the braze weld deposit
- the cast strength of the 'as-cast' filler alloy.

7 Types of solder

7.a and b Solders for soft soldering, hard soldering and brazing

The working principles of solders and their characteristics were discussed in Section 6. In order to distinguish between types of solder for:
- soft soldering (tin–lead solders): tinman's fine or coarse, plumbers' alloys and solder for electrical assemblies
- hard soldering and brazing: filler metals for silver soldering and brazing, brazing brass and copper/zinc alloys

reference should be made to Section 6. There is additional information in the following paragraphs.

7.c The application of British Standards

BS 219: 1977 specifies a range of filler metals used for soft soldering. In the majority of solders the active constituent is tin, which promotes wetting (tinning of the joint). The lead content acts as a dilutant and the ratio of lead to tin determines the melting point.
The addition of antimony increases the creep strength of the alloy.

7.d Forms of supply

The forms of supply are many and varied. The final choice in many cases is dependent on the specific application for which they are to be used.

- **Soft solders**
  For manual soft soldering in general sheet–metal work, stick solders are generally used. For automatic soldering a vast range of preforms is available; these may include washers, discs and wire rings. Resin-cored solders are extensively used in electrical work. Table **7.**1 lists some solders with their applications.
  Solder paint is a uniform mixture of powdered solder and liquid flux, having a creamy consistency, and is applied in the cold state to the joint before heat is applied (Fig. **7.**1).

Fig. **7.**1   Solder paint

Table 7.1 Soft solder selection

BS 219	Chemical composition %			Melting range °C	Application
	Tin	Lead	Antimony		
A	64	35.4	0.6	183–185	Electrical work
F	50	49.5	0.5	183–212	Sheet–metal work
G	40	59.6	0.4	183–234	Capillary fittings
J	30	69.7	0.3	183–255	Plumber's solder

- **Brazing alloys**
  Brazing alloys in rod or wire form can be obtained flux-coated. Preform shapes to suit specific applications may take the form of washers, discs and wire rings and these may, if required, be flux-coated.
- **Filler metals for brazing**
  British Standard 1845: 1984 specifies a range of filler metals used for brazing. The filler metals are grouped as shown in Table **7**.2.

WARNING

Some of the filler metals listed in Table 7.2 may contain cadmium and these can during brazing produce fumes which, if inhaled, are dangerous to health. Precautions should therefore be taken, i.e., ensure good ventilation and wear a face mask.

Table 7.2 Brazing alloy selection

	Parent metal to be brazed	Melting range (°C)	Filler metals
AL	Aluminium, Aluminium alloys	535– 595	Aluminium brazing, filler metals
AG	Copper, copper base alloys	620– 970	Silver brazing filler metals
CP	Copper	645– 740	Copper phosphorys brazing filler metals
CU	Ferrous metals	1045–1085	Copper brazing filler metals
CZ	Copper, Ferrous metals	885– 980	Copper zinc brazing filler metals
NK	Heat resistant alloy and steel	875–1150	Nickel and cobalt base brazing filler metals
PD	Palladium-bearing metals	805–1235	Palladium bearing brazing filler metals
AU	Gold-bearing alloys	905– 990	Gold-bearing brazing filler metals

8 Purpose and types of flux

8.a Formation of oxides

Metal surfaces become more reactive to oxygen when they are heated. To prevent this oxidation during the soldering process a suitable flux is applied to the surfaces being joined. The flux should possess the following characteristics:

- forms a liquid film over the joint and excludes the gases in the atmosphere
- prevents any further oxidation during the heating cycle
- assists in dissolving the oxide film on the metal surface and the solder
- is displaced from the joint by liquid filler metal.

8.b Liquidity of the solder

One of the essentials for obtaining a good joint is the ability of the solder to spread over the joint faces. Any oxide present on the joint faces will inhibit this wetting and spreading of the solder. The function of the flux is to remove the bulk of the oxide and so expose the clean metal over which the solder can flow readily.

8.c Wetting

After preparation, wetting is the next stage in the soldering operation and without it there can be no soldering action. Wetting is that process whereby, after the liquid flux has cleaned any oxide film from the joint surfaces, the solder forms a covering film on the surface rather than rolling off the surface.

8.d Corrosive and non-corrosive fluxes (soft soldering)

Fluxes for soft soldering are often classified into two groups, corrosive or acid fluxes and non-corrosive fluxes (Table **8.**1). The flux can be applied separately, or as a constituent within the solder. Fluxes may take the form of a liquid, paste or solid, and the application for which they are being used will govern the type selected.

Corrosive (acid) fluxes
These are used where conditions require a rapidly working and highly active flux. The common acid fluxes are listed below.
WARNING   These fluxes can cause burns to flesh and clothing. Protect the eyes with goggles and wear rubber gloves and apron when using a corrosive flux.

Zinc chloride (ZnCl), commonly called *killed spirits*, is used on general sheet-metal work. This may be obtained commercially as 'Baker's Soldering Fluid' (Fig. **8.**1).

Ammonium chloride (NH$_4$Cl), commonly called *sal ammoniac*, is used in block form for cleaning the face of the soldering bit before tinning, or in powdered form with zinc chloride, for tinning cast iron.

Hydrochloric acid (HCl) is used in the raw state for pickling the surfaces of the metal and rendering them clean. As a flux it is extremely active and is suitable for soldering zinc and galvanised mild steel. Flux residues of acid fluxes remain active after soldering and will cause corrosion unless removed by thorough cleansing, first in a weak solution – caustic soda – and then in water.

Non-corrosive (passive) fluxes
Passive fluxes are divided into natural resins and tallow.

- **Natural resin** dissolved in suitable organic solvents is the closest approximation to a non-corrosive flux and is particularly suitable for use in the electrical industry (Fig. **8.**2).

Fig. **8.**1   Zinc chloride flux in trade packs

- **Tallow** is used by the plumber for the jointing of lead sheet and pipes. Similar to resin, it is only slightly active when heated to the temperature of the soldering process.

Fig. **8.2**   Resin-based flux in trade packs

Table **8.**1 Fluxes and their application

Flux	Flux type	Material
Hydrochloric acid	Corrosive	Zinc galvanised mild steel
Zinc chloride	Corrosive	Plain carbon steel Brass Copper Tin-plate Terne plate
Phosphoric acid	Corrosive	Stainless steel
Tallow	Non-corrosive	Lead sheet or pipe
Resin-cored solder Resin paste	Non-corrosive	Electrical connections

8.e Fluxes for hard soldering and brazing

When brazing is carried out in air, irrespective of the type of parent metal or brazing alloy used, a flux is required in all cases but one. The exception is the copper–phosphorus brazing alloys, which are self-fluxing when used to braze copper.

It is essential that the correct type of flux is selected for the particular application, since fluxes are only active over a particular temperature range and are ineffective if used outside that range (Table 8.2).

Flux removal

It is essential that all flux residues are removed, since they can present a corrosion hazard. The method of removal will be determined by the type of flux used, but will entail the use of one or a combination of the following:

- a solution of caustic soda
- a solution of sulphuric acid
- a supply of warm water
- physical abrasion.

Table **8.**2 Flux type and temperature range

Type	Temperature range °C
Borax and fluoroborate	Above 750
Fluoride	Below 750
Alkali halide	Below 580

9 Advantages and disadvantages of soldering and brazing

In this section the merits of soft soldering, hard soldering and brazing are considered and presented in a form that will help the student to select the most appropriate method for a particular application.

9.a Soft soldering – advantages and disadvantages

9.a.i Advantages
- *Fluid tight joints are produced.* This is not so with riveted, grooved and knocked up joints.
- *Minimum distortion* to the joined surfaces is caused. There is no hammering, bending or use of excessive heat – factors which can lead to distortion.
- *Few tools* are needed to complete a soldered joint: a soldering iron, a source of heat for a directly heated iron, an electricity supply for an indirectly heated iron, flux, solder and material to clean the joint surfaces and soldering iron bit.
- *Dissimilar metals* may be joined by soft soldering. It is possible to join copper to brass, copper to steel, tin-plate to copper, lead to steel and many other combinations of metals. Soldering of aluminium, however, is very difficult because of the refractory oxide which forms on the surface.
- *Low temperatures* are involved in the soft soldering process. The possibility of any distortion as a result of heat is therefore greatly reduced and the risks of fire or serious accidents involving burns are very much less than they are when hard soldering or brazing.

9.a.ii Disadvantages
- *The relatively low tensile strength* of soft solder has the effect of reducing the overall tensile strength of the material to be joined to that of the solder (refer to Section 6.d). For example, it is possible to join low carbon steel sheets, with a tensile strength of 430 N/mm², with solder. Clearly, however, this would not be practicable, since the tensile strength of the complete fabrication would be reduced to that of the solder, i.e. 53 N/mm².
- *The type of joint used is limited* to lap joints, since a soft solder joint depends on capillary attraction

to cause the solder to flow through a joint. Even when making electrical connections using soft solder, a type of lap joint must be made, since an end-to-end joint in cable would be impracticable.
- *The limited compatibility of some metals* with the soldering agent is another disadvantage. The incompatibility of a tin–lead solder with aluminium is an example. See Section 9.a.i, 'Dissimilar metals'.
- *The joint has a low melting point* which limits the use of soft solder to applications where the working temperature will not rise to much more than 100°C, since, if the temperature of the melting point of the solder was reached, the joint would be breached.

9.b Hard or silver soldering – compared with soft soldering

9.b.i Advantages
- *Greater tensile strength* in the joint is achieved with a hard soldered joint. Table 6.4 lists a number of hard solders, all having a greater tensile strength than soft solders.
- *Fine working* in hard solder is possible because of its greater fluidity. This makes a hard solder particularly suitable for use in jewellery manufacture.
- *The ability to withstand higher working temperatures* than soft solders makes hard solders particularly suitable for use where the temperature at the joint area is likely to be three to four times that which a soft soldered joint could withstand without melting.
- A *wider range of applications* is possible when a hard solder is used instead of a soft solder. As well as the obvious increase in range, because of the advantages listed above, a hard solder can be used for joining dissimilar metals and is more resistant to corrosion under normal conditions than is soft solder.

9.b.ii Disadvantages
- *When parent metal and solder melting temperatures are similar* a joint is difficult to complete. It is a requirement for a soldered joint that the parent metal does not reach a liquid state.

- *The flux residue* is sometimes difficult to remove and requires softening with water unless, before the joint is cooled, it is quenched with cold water; this action sometimes causes the flux residue to crack off. Otherwise immersion in hot agitated water is necessary while brushing off the residue.
- *There is a greater possibility of distortion* because more heat is used when hard soldering than when soft soldering. This risk, however, may be reduced by careful heating and by the use of some form of heat sink.

9.c Brazing – compared with soft and hard soldering

9.c.i Advantages
- *The joint is stronger* when a copper–zinc brazing alloy is used than when a joint is made with soft solder. However, the joint is not as strong as a silver soldered joint.
- *The range of applications* is wider than is the case with soft soldered joints. The applications possible for brazed joints are much the same as with hard or silver soldered joints. One brazing alloy used when brazing copper is copper–phosphorus. An advantage of using this alloy is that it does not need the application of a flux to make the joint. The phosphorus content acts as a deoxidiser during the brazing process.
- *The working temperature range* for a brazed joint is higher than that for soft soldered or hard soldered joints. A fabrication joined by the brazing process is, therefore, able to withstand higher temperatures about the completed joint without the risk of the joint melting.
- *Lower material cost* than hard soldering. The cost of the silver solder alloy is more than that of copper–zinc brazing alloy. However, this is a qualified advantage, since the overall cost of making a hard or silver soldered joint need not be more than that of a brazed joint, because the amount of silver solder alloy used in the joint would be less than the amount of copper–zinc alloy used in the brazed joint.

9.c.ii Disadvantages
- *The higher temperature* required to make a brazed joint has the following effects:
(a) the number of metals which may be readily joined is reduced; this particularly affects the brazing of brass components
(b) Higher energy costs are incurred, since the melting range of brazing alloy is between 860°C and 950°C and therefore more heat is required to melt the filler alloy than is the case with soft and hard soldering.

- *The possibility of distortion* being introduced is greater than in soft or hard soldering because of the higher temperatures used in the brazing process.
- *Removal of flux residue* is sometimes difficult and should be carried out as described in Section 9.b.ii (removal of flux residue after hard soldering). However, some fluxes are insoluble in water and in these cases the components should be immersed in a 10 per cent solution of sulphuric acid, followed by brushing in a jet of warm water. (Refer to safety precautions Section 12.)

9.d Braze welding

The advantages and disadvantages of braze welding have been included here in order that the student may be made aware of the possibility of using this process when working with cast iron components. The subject treatment here differs from that employed in Sections 9.a to 9.c in that the advantages and disadvantages are stated more briefly in tabular format.

Table 9.1 Advantages and disadvantages of braze welding

Advantages	Disadvantages
Process may be carried out in all positions — including overhead.	Because the temperatures required range from 875°C to 910°C there is a risk of distortion (as indeed there is with brazing).
Unlike brazing, it does not rely on capillary attraction.	
Fillet joints may be made.	
A large variety of metals may be joined by this process (Figs. **9**.1, and **9**.2 a and b).	
Particularly suited to the repair of cast iron components (Fig. **9**.3).	
Suitable for the positional welding of copper piping.	
The process can be used for the reclamation of worn parts such as gear teeth, valve seats and bearings (Fig. **9**.4).	

Fig. **9.**1   Gauges and fittings welded to copper pipes

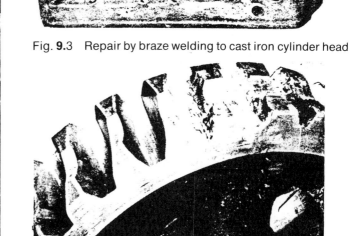

Fig. **9.**3   Repair by braze welding to cast iron cylinder head

Fig. **9.**4   Reclamation of gear teeth by braze welding

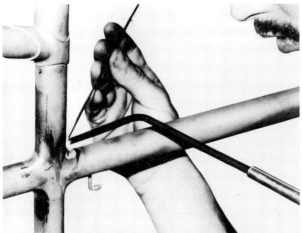

Fig. **9.**2a   Branch pipes being braze welded

Fig. **9.**2b   Copper water cylinder being brazed

Notes on braze welding

● When repairs are to be undertaken to cast iron some pre-heating is required, perhaps up to 400°C, dependent on the size and thickness of the casting.

● Because a braze weld is strong in shear it is important that the contact area between parent metal and filler alloy is as large as possible. In order to obtain this large contact area the joint preparation should be as shown in Fig. **9.**5.

● A technique recommended by Sifbronze Ltd is shown in Fig. **9.**6.

Fig. **9.**5   Shear V edge preparation for the braze welding of cast iron

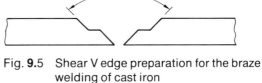

Fig. **9.**6   Sifbronzing technique

10 Positioning and holding of joints

Before any soldering or brazing process is carried out the parts to be joined must be located correctly and accurately. There are a number of aids which may be used to position and hold the component parts while soldering and brazing. Whichever aid is selected to satisfy the requirements of the work in hand, it is important to ensure that the surfaces of the work-piece are not damaged in any way.

10.a Wire and shims

One of the simplest forms of holding devices is soft iron wire. Fig. **10.**1 shows soft iron wire being used to hold two components together for soldering. A shim is used as a distance piece between two mating parts and, in the case of soldering and brazing, when the joint faces are clamped together it may be used to provide the small gap necessary for capillary action to take place. The shim should be of the same material as the component itself except in circumstances described below.

Shims made of filler alloy are sometimes used in the location of parts. In such cases they serve a dual purpose; to assist in location and to supply the brazing filler alloy in the form of an insert.

10.b Ancillary locating and holding devices

10.b.i Spigot joint

One method which is used to locate and hold parts is to form a spigot joint as shown in Fig. **10.**2.
This type of joint may be made either by feeding the filler alloy to the joint in the form of a rod as shown, or by using an insert of filler alloy.

10.b.ii Use of studs and locating pins

- *Studs* are used as follows: One end is threaded and screwed into one of the component parts; the un-screwed end fits into a hole in the other component part and ensures accurate positioning (Fig. **10.**3).
- *Locating pins* are used in a similar way to dowels and have plain ends which fit into a hole in each component part to be joined.

- With either of the above methods, inserts of filler alloy may be used and fitted during the assembly. The material from which the locating pins are made must be the same as is used to make the component parts or be at least compatible with the filler alloy, if a sound joint is to be made.

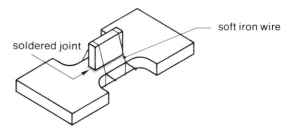

Fig. **10.**1 Soft iron wire holding pieces in place for soldering

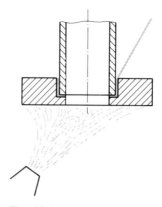

Fig. **10.**2 Location for brazing using a spigot joint

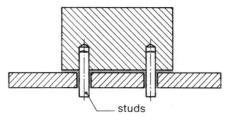

Fig. **10.**3 Location for brazing using studs

Fig. **10**.4   Magnetic clamps

a

b

Fig. **10**.6   A screw clamp in different applications

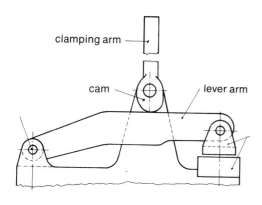

a Cam action clamp

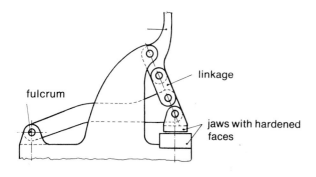

b Toggle action clamp

Fig. **10**.5   Common clamps

10.b.iii Magnetic clamps

Magnetic clamping devices are available in a variety of forms and are used to hold the respective parts together for soldering or brazing. However, as non-ferrous metals are non-magnetic, this type of clamp may only be used with ferrous metals. An exception to this is stainless steel, which although it consists mainly of iron is non-magnetic. Fig. **10**.4 shows two types of magnetic clamp which are available.

10.b.iv Toggle clamps

Toggle clamps incorporate a cam system and provide a pressure contact on the component (Fig. **10**.5b). When they are used on copper or other soft metals care must be taken to avoid damage to the surface of the component.

10.b.v Screw clamp

A clamping device which is suitable for holding angle channel and tubular sections is shown in Fig. **10**.6. The clamp is operated by a screw thread; the face of the clamp can be swivelled to ensure good contact with the workpiece.

10.b.vi Versatile clamp

A versatile clamp used for holding various sections, including pipes, is shown in Fig. 10.7b.

The jaws of this clamp may be moved along the bar quickly until they are in contact with the work. By tightening the tee-handle screw the locking action is brought into play. Increased flexibility of application is provided because the jaws are able to accept differently shaped workholding adaptors.

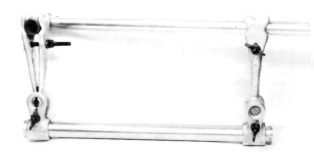

Fig. 10.8   Pipe clamp

a Special purpose clamping

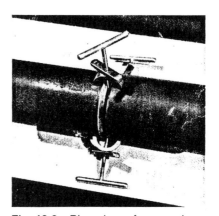

Fig. 10.9   Pipe clamp for use where space is limited

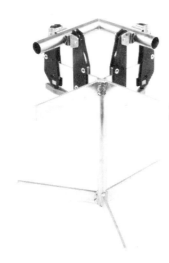

b Multi-purpose clamp (jig)

Fig. 10.7   Versatile clamps used for various shaped sections and parts

10.b.vii Universal clamp

The clamp shown in Fig. 10.8 is suitable for holding pipes of up to 50 mm outside diameter. It is fitted with ball joint clips that can hold two pipes to any position, and is suitable for use when soldering or brazing pipes. Fig. 10.9 shows a pipe clamp used in locations where space is limited.

To make a satisfactory joint by the soldering or brazing processes certain rules of planning and procedure must be observed. These rules can be grouped together under two main headings, as set out and discussed below.

11.a Planning and preparation

The first thing that must be decided is what technique is to be used to make the joint. Is it to be soldered or is it to be brazed? The advantages and disadvantages of each technique are discussed in Section 9.

11.a.i Cleanliness of the joint

The joint surfaces must be thoroughly cleaned before any soldering or brazing can be attempted.

11.a.ii Positioning the joint

The parts to be joined must be held securely in position during the joining operation. A description of some securing devices is given in Section 10.

11.a.iii Conservation of heat

Soldering and brazing processes use heat energy which is costly to provide. It follows, therefore, that any method of preventing excessive heat loss from the workpiece during the joining operation, provided it does not inhibit the manipulation of the joining tools, is to be encouraged. In Section 5 the use of a firebrick to conserve heat is discussed.

11.a.iv Selection of the correct filler alloy

The choice of filler alloy is basic to the production of a good joint. Tables 6.1, 6.2, 6.3 and 6.4 list the common solders, brazing brasses and silver solders and provide a guide to their use.

11.a.v Choice of flux

The correct flux must be used. Section 8 should be consulted for guidance in the choice. However, it cannot be too strongly stressed that where a corrosive flux is used great care must be taken to ensure that all traces are removed after the joining operation. **If electrical connections are to be made then a resin flux must be used.**

11.a.vi Choice of heating method

The choice of the method of heating will depend on a number of factors: size and thickness of the parts to be joined and the number to be joined at any one time. Section 5 should be consulted and the appropriate method selected accordingly.

11.a.vii Tinning the parent metal

Certain metals can cause some difficulty when soft soldering is attempted. To overcome this the edges to be joined must be 'tinned' before assembly.

11.b Carrying out the joining operation

11.b.i Tinning the soldering iron

To ensure that there is an efficient transfer of heat from the soldering iron to the workpiece and to facilitate the flow of solder the soldering iron bit must be tinned (refer to Section 5).

11.b.ii Cleanliness

If dirt and grease are present the joint cannot be made. Ensure that neither of these enters or remains in the joint area during the soldering operation by working continuously and efficiently.

11.b.iii Application of the flux

The flux must be applied evenly over the whole surface area of the joint.

11.b.iv Distribution of heat

An even distribution of heat over the area to be joined is required. Too much localised heat will cause overheating and lead to a poor joint in the case of soldering, or to distortion or even melting of the parent metal in the case of brazing.

11.b.v Applications of solder

38   Only a thin film of solder is required to ensure a good joint (refer to Section 6.d). The solder must always be kept in a fluid state during the soldering process, therefore the soldering iron must always be kept sufficiently hot to maintain the temperature at the joint.

12 Safety precautions

As has been mentioned in the introduction to this book, almost all soldering and brazing operations are hazardous and so demand safety precautions. Those outlined below are specific to the various tasks involved. The student is recommended to consult the series book *Observing Safe Practices and Moving Loads* for more general guidance. Essentially, all operations should follow a *safe system of work, under adequate supervision.*

12.a Compressed gas equipment

Stringent safety precautions must be observed at all times. There is always some element of danger when gases are stored under compression.

12.a.i Identification of gases

Industrial gases are identified by the colour of the cylinder in which they are stored. BS 349: 1973 lists the cylinder colours:
- oxygen – black
- acetylene – maroon
- air – grey

Note: Natural gas is not normally supplied in cylinders, as piped gas is available.

12.a.ii Assembly of compressed gas equipment

To avoid confusion when assembling the equipment the threads on the securing unions are threaded differently for fuel gases and non-fuel gases:
- fuel gases (acetylene) – left-hand threaded
- non-fuel gases (oxygen, air) – right-hand threaded.

12.a.iii Storage of cylinders

When compressed gas is stored the following precautions should be observed.
- Never store oxygen and acetylene gas cylinders in the same room.
- Lighting fitments used in storerooms must be flameproof.
- Storerooms must be well ventilated with ventilation ports at both ceiling and floor levels.

- Acetylene cylinders should be stored in the upright position (Fig. **12.**1).
- If the cylinders are stored in the open they must be shaded from the sun and protected from ice and snow.
- Never store cylinders near any source of heat (Fig. **12.**2).

Store acetylene cylinders in a cool dry place away from heat and direct sunlight. Do not mix with oxygen cylinders. Switches and lamps must be flameproof.

Fig. **12.**1   Storage of acetylene cylinders

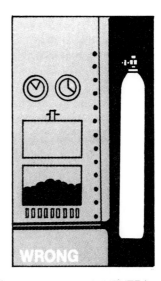

Fig. **12.**2   Gas cylinders should NEVER be placed near a heat source

- Never allow grease or oil to come into contact with oxygen cylinders (Fig. **12**.3).

12.a.iv Handling cylinders

- Do not handle oxygen cylinders with greasy hands or allow an oily cloth to be used to wipe them down.
- Avoid leakage; a small leak of acetylene and oxygen in a confined space could lead to an explosion. Test for leaks with a brush and a soap solution (Fig. **12**.4).
- Never use copper pipes in a situation where acetylene may come into contact with them, e.g. couplings between cylinders, because copper and acetylene can combine chemically to cause a breakdown of the copper.
- Never allow cylinders to clash together.
- Never use chains to hoist cylinders (Fig. **12**.5); use a rope sling. If more than one cylinder is to be hoisted at a time a specially designed cradle with a chain suspension should be used.

12.b Working in confined spaces

If possible, always avoid working in a confined space. This is not always practicable and in these circumstances fresh air must be supplied to the operator. Air can be ducted in and circulated by pumps. Never use oxygen to ventilate a confined space.

12.c Fluxes

Acid fluxes are used when soldering. As has been pointed out, these fluxes are corrosive and great care must be taken to avoid contact with them. The eyes are particularly vulnerable to damage from acids. The following precautions should be taken.
- Always wear safety glasses or a visor.
- Always apply a barrier cream to the hands before commencing the soldering operation.

Alkali fluxes are used in the brazing process; these fluxes can also cause irritation to the eyes and skin and the precautions listed above should also be observed when brazing.

12.d Electrical hazards

To avoid hazards, electrical equipment used in the soldering and brazing processes should be frequently inspected for electrical safety by a qualified electrician. Operators should bring to the notice of

Fig. **12**.3   Oxygen cylinders must never be stored next to oil or grease

Fig. **12**.4   Checking for leaks

Fig. **12**.5   Never use chains to lift gas cylinders

the foreman or supervisor any of the following:
- loose connections
- frayed cables
- broken plugs
- broken or loose electrical fittings.

12.e Fire prevention

It is always better to prevent a fire from starting than to deal with one once it has started. The following precautions must be observed.
- Brazing stations should be insulated from flammable materials by using suitable refractory materials.
- A torch should always be pointed away from the operator when being lit.
- When the gas mixture produces a non-luminous flame extra special care must be taken.

12.e.i Lighting up procedure for hand torches

- Switch on the fuel gas at supply.
- Switch on the oxygen or compressed air at supply.
- Open the fuel gas valve on the torch, allow the gas to flow for two to three seconds to ensure that all air has been exhausted from the torch body.
- Light the torch and adjust oxygen or compressed air valve on the torch to give the type of flame required.
- Always turn the gases off when the torch is put down after finishing the joint. The oxygen or air should always be turned off before the gas supply.

12.e.ii Fires in electrical equipment

In the case of an electrical fire, i.e. a fire in an electrical machine, always switch off the electricity supply before attempting to extinguish the fire.

It is very important that the correct type of extinguisher is used on an electrical fire. **Water must never be used on live electrical equipment and since foam contains water this must not be used either.**
- Halons are used on fires involving live electrical equipment. Halons form a dense cloud of non-flammable vapour on the burning mass, limiting the air supply and interfering with the spread of the flame. However, they are toxic and should be used with care.
  Note: Halon is the trade name for the liquid chemical extinguishers which are halogenated hydrocarbons. *Halon 1301* is colourless, odourless and is electrically non-conductive.
- A carbon dioxide gas extinguisher, painted BLACK, may also be used on live electrical

equipment. It smothers the burning mass and limits the air supply. It also has the advantage of avoiding contamination of the electrical equipment, which can occur if a dry powder is used as the extinguisher.

12.e.iii Chemical fires

Fires involving flammable liquids such as petrol, oil, fat, solvents or paint should be extinguished by using a smothering action. **Water should never be used**, since this would only serve to float the burning liquid and spread the fire.

Two types of extinguisher are recommended: foam extinguishers painted CREAM and dry powder extinguishers painted BLUE.

12.f Purging of vessels

When all flammable material is driven out of a tank, drum or vessel either by the use of steam or an inert gas, the operation is known as 'purging'.

The following text describes procedures requiring practical knowledge and experience. It cannot be stressed too strongly that because of the hazards present, the soldering or brazing of vessels which contain, or have contained, flammable or noxious liquids or gases should *not* be undertaken other than in workshop or controlled conditions and under skilled supervision. Fig. **12.**6 shows the result of an attempt to solder an unpurged petrol tank. Wherever practical, the flammable materials should be removed completely before any welding, brazing or soldering is carried out. There are two main methods

Fig. **12.**6   Result of a soldering iron being applied to an unpurged petrol tank

used to remove flammable material from a tank or drum:

- steaming out
- boiling in water containing alkali or detergents.

12.f.i Steaming out

All filler caps, drain plugs or other fittings should be removed from the tank. After the tank is emptied steam at low pressure is introduced into it. The condensate must be able to drain away. The time required for steaming out varies, but should be carried out for at least thirty minutes.

To prevent the build-up of static electricity during the steaming out of large tanks, the tank and the steam pipe should both be earthed, and the steam pipe should be electrically bonded to the tank.

12.f.ii Boiling out

Boiling out is accomplished by immersing the tank or drum in boiling water, ensuring that the boiling water can enter the drum. The water should be kept at boiling point while the tank is immersed. The time spent on this operation should be at least thirty minutes.

12.f.iii Testing

Before any work is carried out after the purging operations, tests must be carried out by using explosimeters to ensure that no residual flammable material remains. These tests must be undertaken by a responsible person who is familiar with the dangers involved.

12.f.iv Continuous purging with work in progress

In some cases, steam purging is not completely successful. In these circumstances steam should be passed through continually while 'hot-work' is being carried out. In this way an inert atmosphere substantially free from air is maintained in the tank and any trace of flammable vapour set free during the work cannot be ignited within the vessel. Other procedures involve the use of nitrogen or carbon dioxide as the inert gas. Carbon dioxide may also be used in the form of 'dry ice' (solid carbon dioxide).

12.g Safety guards, protective clothing and equipment

No person under eighteen years of age shall work at any prescribed dangerous machine unless he or she:

- has received sufficient training to ensure safe working
- is under adequate supervision to ensure safe working.

A list of prescribed dangerous machines can be found in the *Schedule to the Dangerous Machines (Training of Young Persons) Order* 1954.

12.g.i Safety guards

Where possible a fixed guard should always be fitted so as to enclose the danger point or points on a machine. The guarding should be fixed in such a manner that a special tool is needed to remove it.

Other types of guarding systems in use include:

- *Interlocking guards* which connect in such a way that when they are removed the control circuit is broken and the machine cannot be started.
- *Automatic guards* which ensure the operational safety of the worker by physically excluding him from the danger area, as in the case of a power press.
- *Proximity guards* which actuate a mechanical safety sequence when the worker is in close proximity to the danger point.

12.g.ii Protective clothing

Protective clothing should always be worn in the workshop. When processes involving heat are being used the clothing should be flame-resistant. Where there is a risk of damage to eyes, either from the glare of a flame or from some form of spatter, then the correct protective glasses must be worn.

Heat-retardant gloves should be worn to protect the hands from burns.

Adequate footwear must always be worn in the workshop.

12.h Personal hygiene

The soldering and brazing processes involve the use of contaminants. It is most important that:

- hands are thoroughly cleaned after working
- nails are kept cut short
- long hair is tied back and covered
- any cuts and abrasions on the skin are kept clean and covered
- food and drink are not consumed at the work station.

BACKGROUND TO TECHNOLOGY

SUBJECT MATTER OF SECTIONS 1-8

SECTION 1
Basic Physical Quantities, Electricity and Magnetism

1   Introduction to the SI system
2   Structure and states of matter
3   Mass, force and weight
4   Mass per unit volume
5   Basic theory of electricity
6   Circuits
7   Magnetism

SECTION 2
Forces

1   Effects of force
2   Resultant and equilibrant forces
3   Resolution of forces
4   Moments; the theorem of moments
5   Conditions of equilibrium
6   Centre of gravity; equilibrium and stability
7   Friction

SECTION 3
Pressure

1   Pressure
2   Pressure exerted by liquids
3   Pressure in gases
4   Pressure on liquids
5   Connected vessels
6   Upthrust

SECTION 4
Heat

1   Heat and energy
2   Melting and solidifying
3   Evaporation and condensation
4   Dissolving and solidifying
5   Heat transfer

SECTION 5
Thermal Movement

1   Temperature
2   Thermal movement of solids
3   Thermal movement of liquids
4   Thermal movement of gases
5   The gas laws

SECTION 6
Motion

1   Linear motion at uniform velocity
2   Rotation at uniform speed
3   Direct transmission
4   Indirect transmission
5   Uniform acceleration from rest
6   Uniform acceleration and deceleration

SECTION 7
Energy

1   Force, mass and acceleration
2   Work
3   Power; rating and efficiency of machines
4   Potential and kinetic energy
5   Centripetal and centrifugal force

SECTION 8
Principles of tool construction; materials technology

1   Tools using the lever principle
2   Tools based on the pulley
3   Inclined plane and hydraulic equipment
4   Materials subject to tension and compression
5   Materials subject to shear

Note

All the books of 'Technology of Skilled Processes' are in one way or another related to the series 'Background to Technology'. In the case of 'Soft Soldering, Hard Soldering and Brazing' the sections 1.2, 4.1, 4.2, 4.3, 4.4, 4.5, 5.1, 5.2, 5.3 and 5.4 must be studied and will be examined.

Information about the Syllabus and the books of Background to Technology can be obtained from
The City and Guilds of London Institute,
76 Portland Place,
Londen W1N4 AA
or from the Publisher of these books Stam Press, Ltd,
Old Station Drive,
Leckhampton
Cheltenham GL53 0DN

Technology of Skilled Processes

Basic Engineering
Competences 201

Soft Soldering, Hard Soldering and Brazing

Practice and test questions

Published as a
co-operative venture
between
Stam Press Ltd

and

City and Guilds

Practice and test questions

The questions in this book are intended to help the student achieve and demonstrate a knowledge and understanding of the subject matter covered by this book. Accordingly, the questions follow the original section order, under the same headings. Finally there are questions spanning the sections and approximating to the level of those in the relevant examination of the City and Guilds of London Institute.

FOR THE ATTENTION OF THE TEACHER AND THE STUDENT

The content of this book and the questions for the student have been carefully prepared by a group of special editors in co-operation with the City and Guilds of London Institute. We should like to draw your attention to the copyright clause shown at the beginning of the book, on this page and the following pages:

First published in Great Britain 1987
as a co-operative venture between Stam Press Ltd and the City and Guilds of London Institute

Reprinted 1989

© Stam Press Ltd, Cheltenham 1987

Printed and bound in Great Britain by
Martin's of Berwick

SOFT SOLDERING, HARD SOLDERING AND BRAZING

Name: _____ Class: _____ Number: _____

1 Soldering and brazing

The following questions relate to the above subject, but what is said here about answering them *also* applies to similarly framed questions covering the later subject headings.

Questions like 1 and 2 provide a number of possible answers, usually four, lettered a, b, c and d. Unless otherwise indicated, only *one* is correct. You are required to decide which it is and circle the appropriate letter, as shown in the example below.

Example

The principal constituents of a soft solder are:

a   lead and copper

b   copper and silver

ⓒ lead and tin

d   tin and silver

Other questions require you to answer in short clear statements. If you are asked to produce a sketch, make sure that it is clearly labelled.

---

1   The melting point of a filler alloy used for soft soldering is usually:

   a   below 100°C

   b   between 180°C and 280°C

   c   between 210°C and 350°C

   d   above 300°C

---

2   The melting point of a filler alloy used for brazing is usually:

   a   above 500°C

   b   between 350°C and 550°C

   c   above 1000°C

   d   100°C below the melting point of the metal to be joined

---

3   State the meaning of the term 'hard soldering'.

---

4   State FIVE characteristics that a joint produced by soft or hard soldering must have.

---

2 Methods used

The following questions relate to the above subject. Except where otherwise indicated, the correct answers should be given as explained above.

---

1   List THREE items of equipment used when making a soft soldered joint.

---

2   State what is generally understood by 'the use of indirect heat' in relation to soldering and brazing.

SOFT SOLDERING, HARD SOLDERING AND BRAZING

Name: _____ Class: _____ Number: _____

3 Brazing is well within the scope of a DIY enthusiast. List the brazing equipment likely to be found in a DIY workshop.

_____
_____
_____
_____

4 For industrial brazing procedures sophisticated equipment is used. Name TWO such items of equipment.

_____
_____
_____
_____

3 Forms of heating and heating equipment used

The following questions relate to the above subject. Except where otherwise indicated, the correct answers should be given as explained on page 47.

1 A joint area cools while a directly heated soldering iron is being reheated. State how this problem can be overcome.

_____
_____
_____

2 Use a clearly labelled sketch to describe the construction of an electric soldering iron.

3 Copper is used as the soldering 'bit' because:
a   it is cheap
b   it has a high melting temperature
c   it has high thermal conductivity
d   it retains heat for long periods

4 Name a gas mixture used when brazing.

_____
_____

5 State ONE method by which heat can be conserved when brazing small components. Illustrate with a simple sketch.

_____
_____

6 State briefly how heat is generated on the surface of the components to be joined during HF induction heating.

_____
_____
_____

SOFT SOLDERING, HARD SOLDERING AND BRAZING

Name: _____ Class: _____ Number: _____

7 State the meaning of 'a reducing atmosphere'.

_____

_____

8 When a furnace is used to complete the brazing process, the components must be:
  a   pre-fluxed, positioned and assembled with a filler alloy insert
  b   cleaned and placed within the furnace well apart from any other component
  c   assembled and ready for the application of flux and filler alloy when the required temperature is reached
  d   surrounded by a reducing atmosphere

4 Applications of soldering and brazing

The following questions relate to the above subject. Except where otherwise indicated, the correct answers should be given as explained on page 47.

1 State THREE applications of soft soldering.

_____

_____

2 State why, in fabrication work, hard soldering or brazing might be preferred to welding.

_____

_____

3 A carbide tip is secured to a cutting tool by:
  a   soldering using a special flux
  b   brazing
  c   soft soldering
  d   fitting in a groove and securing with hard soldered keys

5 Description of equipment, principles of operation and making a joint

The following questions relate to the above subject. Except where otherwise indicated, the correct answers should be given as explained on page 47.

1 State how a soldering iron is prepared for use when required.

_____

_____

_____

2 The figure shows a surface being tinned before a joint is made. Label it to identify:
  a   The oxide film on parent metal
  b   The solidifying solder
  c   The boiling flux removing oxide film

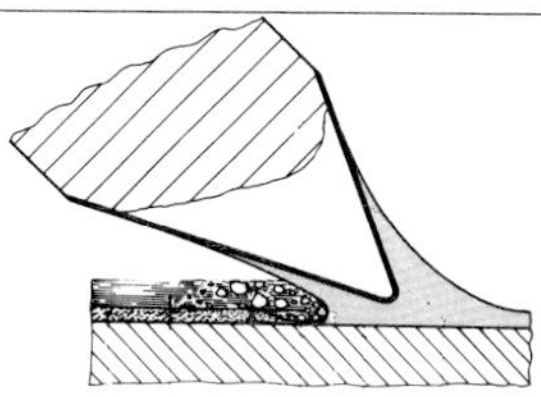

3 State ONE advantage which a braze welded joint has over a brazed joint.

SOFT SOLDERING, HARD SOLDERING AND BRAZING

Name: _____ Class: _____ Number: _____

4   With the aid of a sketch, show how a brass nipple can be soft soldered to a copper pipe when a gas torch flame is being used.

5   State why a soldered joint must always be lapped.

6   Sketch a cross section through a soft soldered lap joint and label it clearly.

7   The figure shows one form of heating in resistance brazing. Add a caption describing which it is and complete the leader lines with their correct labels.

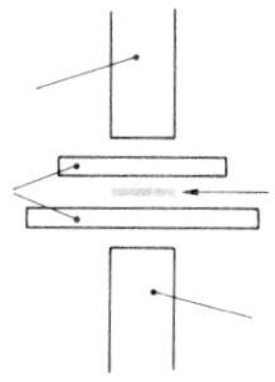

8   State what is meant by intermetallic compound, with reference to soft soldering.

9   State why a thick layer of solder between components is likely to produce a weaker joint.

10   A solution of hydrochloric acid may be used to clean a joint after soft soldering. What precautions must then be taken to ensure that no corrosion takes place?

11   The type of blowpipe flame used in brazing should be:
a   oxidising
b   neutral
c   carbonising
d   carburising

12   State TWO common forms in which soft solder is supplied.

13   State TWO common forms in which brazing filler alloy is supplied.

Name: _____ Class: _____ Number: _____

14 The current frequency of an HF induction furnace is:
   a between 50 Hz and 1 kHz
   b between 400 Hz and 4 kHz
   c between 1 kHz and 1 MHz
   d between 1 kHz and 10 MHz

15 State how the zinc content of the filler metal may cause porosity in a brazed joint.

16 State the type of flux used in braze welding.

17 When a salt bath furnace is used the components to be joined are fully immersed in the liquid salt. This ensures that:
   a the components are subjected to pressure
   b the salt and filler alloy combine to produce a strong joint
   c the components are given a corrosion-proof coating
   d even heating is achieved

18 When the dip brazing technique has been employed the components are sometimes coated with filler alloy. State TWO methods of removing this coating.

19 The depth of heat penetration resulting from HF induction heating is dependent on frequency and time. Describe the difference in depth of penetration when a component is subjected to:
   a a high frequency for a short time
   b a low frequency for a longer period

6 Working principles of soft solders and filler alloys

The following questions relate to the above subject. Except where indicated, the correct answers should be given as explained on page 47.

1 State what is meant by the 'eutectic' temperature of an alloy.

2 The solidification temperature of a common tin/lead alloy is:
   a 120°C
   b 183°C
   c 157°C
   d 198°C

3 State why it is possible to wipe a joint when using plumber's solder.

4 State TWO effects of adding antimony to a soft solder.

SOFT SOLDERING, HARD SOLDERING AND BRAZING

Name: _____ Class: _____ Number: _____

5 Silver, silicon, nickel and manganese are sometimes added to brazing alloys to give certain properties. State the relevant properties against the additives listed below.

a silver _____

b silicon _____

c nickel _____

d manganese _____

6 State how an increase in temperature affects the tensile strength of a soft solder.

_____
_____
_____

7 With the aid of a sketch describe capillary action.

_____
_____

8 Give the limitations there are on the type of solder that may be used when making a joint in a pipe for conveying drinking water.

_____
_____
_____

7 Types of solder

The following questions relate to the above subject. Except where otherwise indicated, the correct answers should be given as explained on page 47.

1 State what is meant by solder paint.

_____
_____

2 In a tin–lead solder one constituent aids 'wetting' and the other is a dilutant. Identify beside a and b which has these properties.

a Tin _____

b Lead _____

_____

3 State the precautions that must be taken when using a brazing alloy containing cadmium.

_____
_____
_____

4 The composition of 'plumber's' solder is:
a 70% tin, 30% lead
b 70% zinc, 30% copper
c 70% copper, 30% zinc
d 70% lead, 30% tin

SOFT SOLDERING, HARD SOLDERING AND BRAZING

Name: _____ Class: _____ Number: _____

8 Purpose and types of flux

The following questions relate to the above subject. Except where otherwise indicated, the correct answers should be given as explained on page 47.

1 State how a flux inhibits oxidation of the surfaces being joined by soldering or brazing.

2 Explain the term 'wetting'.

3 State the TWO main groups into which fluxes are classified.

4 Indicate the type of flux used when making soldered connections in electrical wiring:
   a ammonium chloride
   b resin
   c zinc chloride
   d sal ammoniac

5 Alkali halide is used as a flux when brazing in applications where the temperature used is:
   a below 580°C
   b below 750°C
   c between 750°C and 1000°C
   d above 1000°C

9 Advantages and disadvantages of soldering and brazing

The following questions relate to the above subject. Except where otherwise indicated, the correct answers should be given as explained on page 47.

1 State ONE advantage that a soft soldered joint has over a riveted or a grooved joint.

2 State ONE reason why a hard soldered joint is recommended for use when working with jewellery.

3 State FOUR limitations of soft soldered joints.

SOFT SOLDERING, HARD SOLDERING AND BRAZING

Name: _____ Class: _____ Number: _____

4 State ONE application of a brazed joint.

_____
_____

5 State the reason why energy costs are greater for brazing than for soldering.

_____
_____

6 If a cast iron cylinder-head is to be braze welded the component should be pre-heated to approximately:
a 1000°C
b 200°C
c 400°C
d 500°C

10 Positioning and holding of joints

The following questions relate to the above subject. Except where otherwise indicated, the correct answers should be given as explained on page 47.

1 Show, by means of a sketch, a method – other than using clamps – of holding components together while soldering.

2 Magnetic clamps can be used to hold in position all ferrous metal components with one exception, which is:

_____

3 Shims are sometimes used when components are clamped or held together for brazing. They are made of:
a a neutral material
b a combustible material that will burn away during brazing
c lead
d filler metal

4 State a precaution that must be observed when using toggle clamps to hold copper components.

_____
_____

5 Sketch and clearly label a toggle action clamp.

SOFT SOLDERING, HARD SOLDERING AND BRAZING

Name: _____ Class: _____ Number: _____

11 General rules for efficiency in soldering and brazing

The following questions relate to the above subject. Except where otherwise indicated, the correct answers should be given as explained on page 47.

1 Some metals are difficult to solder. State the surface treatment given to components manufactured from 'difficult to solder' materials.

2 When discussing the making of an essential joint, what is the first decision to be made?

3 State ONE reason why it is necessary to work smoothly and quickly when making a soldered or brazed joint.

12 Safety precautions

The following questions relate to the above subject. Except where otherwise indicated, the correct answers should be given as explained on page 47.

1 Listed below are three identification colours for containers of industrial gases. Look at the list of three gases and beside each write the correct letter, a, b or c to denote the colour of its container.

   a grey   oxygen _____

   b black   acetylene _____

   c maroon   air _____

2 To avoid confusion, different thread directions are used for compressed gas equipment. State the thread configuration for securing unions on:

   a fuel gases _____

   b non-fuel gases _____

3 State the important precautions that must be observed when cleaning oxygen equipment.

4 State the precautions to be observed when using acid fluxes.

SOFT SOLDERING, HARD SOLDERING AND BRAZING

Name: _____ Class: _____ Number: _____

5 What is meant by the term 'purging' in relation to soldering and brazing operations.

_____
_____
_____

6 List the steps you would take to make safe a petrol tank that *must* be repaired by brazing.

_____
_____
_____

SOFT SOLDERING, HARD SOLDERING AND BRAZING

Name: _____ Class: _____ Number: _____

The following questions span the syllabus subject matter and approximate to the level of those in the relevant examination paper of the City and Guilds of London Institute. Answers should be short and clear.

1 The melting point of the filler alloy used for brazing is usually:
   a below 250°C
   b between 250°C and 350°C
   c between 550°C and 950°C
   d above 950°C

2 State how the tensile strength of a brazed joint compares with that of a soft soldered joint.

3 State TWO properties which a soft soldered joint must have.

4 State THREE applications of soft soldering.

5 Indicate which one of the following types of joint is most suitable for soft soldering:
   a single-vee
   b double-vee
   c square butt
   d joggled lap

6 State why a very small gap should be provided for a soft soldered joint.

7 The type of blowpipe flame used for brazing should be:
   a neutral
   b carburising
   c carbonising
   d oxidising

8 Indicate which of the following joining processes depends on capillary attraction:
   a braze welding
   b oxy-acetylene welding
   c manual metal arc welding
   d brazing

9 Give ONE example where furnace brazing is particularly economical when compared with torch brazing.

SOFT SOLDERING, HARD SOLDERING AND BRAZING

Name: _____ Class: _____ Number: _____

10 State TWO advantages of using a salt bath furnace as a source of heat for a brazed joint.

_____

_____

_____

11 State THREE factors that must be considered when selecting a brazing filler alloy.

_____

_____

_____

_____

12 In the resistance brazing process heat is generated by the current and the
    a conductivity of the electrodes
    b conductivity of the plates
    c electrical resistance of the joint
    d electrical resistance of the plates

13 Braze welding is often selected in preference to fusion welding because:
    a it produces a stronger joint
    b the process takes less time to produce a joint
    c the resulting joint is easier to machine
    d more distortion is created

14 State TWO factors which affect the strength of a brazed joint.

_____

_____

_____

15 State which element in a soft solder promotes 'wetting' of the joint.

_____

_____

16 State the type of brazing filler alloy that should be used to make a joint in a copper pipe.

_____

_____

_____

17 The main constituents of a brazing filler alloy are:
    a tin and lead
    b copper and tin
    c copper and zinc
    d tin and zinc

18 A flux is used during brazing in order to:
    a chemically clean the surface
    b prevent corrosion from forming
    c increase the speed of brazing
    d slow down the rate of solidification

19 A suitable flux to use when brazing two components together is one which has a base of:
    a sodium chloride
    b zinc chloride
    c borax
    d sulphuric acid

SOFT SOLDERING, HARD SOLDERING AND BRAZING

Name: _____ Class: _____ Number: _____

20 The main reason for using a non-acid type of flux when soft soldering is to:
 a clean the metal
 b cause an even flow of heat
 c prevent corrosion
 d create a chemical bond

21 Indicate which one of the following is a corrosive acid-type soldering flux:
 a tallow
 b resin
 c zinc chloride
 d petroleum jelly

22 State THREE characteristics that a flux must have when used for soft soldering.

23 State how the flux residue may be removed after the completion of a soft soldered joint.

24 State ONE application of a brazed joint.

25 With the aid of a sketch, show ONE method – other than clamping – of holding two components together whilst they are being joined by brazing.

26 State TWO factors which must be decided before a joint is either hard or soft soldered.

27 State the British Standard identification colour used on:

 a acetylene cylinders _____

 b oxygen cylinders _____

28 State THREE safety precautions that MUST be observed when gas cylinders are stored.

29 State TWO safety precautions that MUST be observed when brazing.

SOFT SOLDERING, HARD SOLDERING AND BRAZING

Name: _____ Class: _____ Number: _____

30 Give the reason why water or foam should never be used on
a fire in electrical equipment.

_____

_____

_____